# The Adventures of Muhammad Smith and The Million Man March

*by*
*Anonymous*

authorHOUSE™

*1663 LIBERTY DRIVE, SUITE 200*
*BLOOMINGTON, INDIANA 47403*
*(800) 839-8640*
*WWW.AUTHORHOUSE.COM*

*This book is a work of fiction. People, places, events, and situations are the product of the author's imagination. Any resemblance to actual persons, living or dead, or historical events, is purely coincidental.*

*© 2005 DCT All Rights Reserved.*

*No part of this book may be reproduced, stored in a retrieval system, or transmitted by any means without the written permission of the author.*

*First published by AuthorHouse 08/08/05*

*ISBN: 1-4208-6704-0 (sc)*

*Printed in the United States of America*
*Bloomington, Indiana*

*This book is printed on acid-free paper.*

***Flowers come from dirt.***

Stevie Livingston, 1995

"Personal! James three weeks ago you were calling me stupid for even thinking about the Million Man March. Now you want a bus for the Black Republicans of Suburban America! I mean Excuuuuse me. Just what is it that you and these Negro republicans hope to find at the Million Man March, a tax write off?"

"Fair question cousin but the best that I can tell you is that I want to hear what he is going to say. I'm hoping he can say what I've never heard before."

"And what would that be Cousin James?"

"God why did you make me Black?"

There were a half a dozen ways to Sunday that Muhammad could of answered that question. Each one of them were nasty and vindictive along the lines of calling someone an Uncle Tom. But Muhammad remained silent.

# Contents

| | | |
|---|---|---|
| Chapter One | Patty Duke | 1 |
| Chapter Two | Ralph Cramden | 10 |
| Chapter Three | Details at Eleven | 24 |
| Chapter Four | Peyton Place | 37 |
| Chapter Five | Perry Mason | 49 |
| Chapter Six | Batman | 57 |
| Chapter Seven | Julia | 71 |
| Chapter Eight | General Hospital | 89 |
| Chapter Nine | Let's Make A Deal | 103 |
| Chapter Ten | Pee Wee's Playhouse | 118 |
| Chapter Eleven | Burger King | 129 |
| Chapter Twelve | The Monkees | 139 |
| Chapter Thirteen | Love, American Style | 151 |
| Chapter Fourteen | This Is Your Life | 164 |
| Chapter Fifteen | The Fresh Prince | 180 |
| Chapter Sixteen | Star Wars | 192 |
| Chapter Seventeen | All In The Family | 217 |
| Chapter Eighteen | Archie Bunker | 235 |
| Chapter Nineteen | Gunsmoke | 253 |

# Dichotomy: PATTY DUKE

Muhammad Charles Smith, complete with Jerry Curl: Negro Extraordinaire, to hear him tell it, but in all reality he was the day manager at the local Fast Food Delite. At the age of 37 this was his success. Far from the success he had seen for years on page five of Ebony Magazine of the 'First Black…to be a doctor in Three Peaks, Alaska'. He had once been given the gift, by his grandmother, of a five year subscription of "How to be the first Black person in Beaumont, Montana". Well actually they were copies of Ebony Magazine, the first Black magazine to be White. A magazine he had hated since childhood, but mothers know best.

It was just after lunch at about 1:30 and the crowd was a little more than the routine 20 orders an hour, far from the surprisingly light but still maddening lunch hour crowd on this Thursday afternoon in Philly PA, in the petite heat of August 1995.

It was August 1995 and OJ Simpson was on trial for his life. He had assembled an impressive team of lawyers and lurking in the background was an impressive retirement fund. Mr. Simpson was prepared. It was odd that Muhammad felt anything for Mr. OJ: An ex-football star, current movie star and the number one, part time football commentator on Network TV. All that and he had a White woman too. OJ was the kind of smart celebrity who never made waves, stayed completely out of politics, race, and anger. It would have been nice to get the occasional "Right On" during the occasional police shooting or the rare Rodney King, like Jim Brown was so quick to do. Funny, two record holding running backs...

...different as night and day.

Meet OJ who's been most everywhere, from CBS to the NFL

BUT JIMMY'S ONLY SEEN THE SIGHTS A BOY CAN SEE FROM GHETTO

FIGHTS

....What a crazy pair!
But they're Negroes,
Identical Negroes and you'll find
They eat alike,
They think alike,
At times they even stink alike.
You can lose your mind
When Negroes are two of a kind.

Yeah that was Jim Brown and OJ Simpson.

That airport jumpin' guy and Jefferson from the Dirty Dozen: A bewitching dichotomy that always existed in Muhammad's Black World. The classic explanation was the house Nigger and the field hand from slavery days. Two claimed entities. It was claimed that there was the Negro who embraced the European culture of perfection as was the case for our now beloved OJ Simpson. Then there was the Negro who held on to whatever culture they could find in repudiation of all things European, even their theories of perfection, to the point of sacrifice ala Jim Brown. Muhammad Charles Smith often thought that this insidious dichotomy was not a conflict between individuals but a schizophrenia from within.

Big words he dared not use in the common company of the employees of Fast Food Delite. Thoughts he kept to himself. But one thing he did share with his fellow burger flippers was an attraction to OJ Simpson and the 'funny' feelings he felt for the House Nigger, du jour. Mr. OJ Simpson married White, jobbed white and complete with big eyes in the movies: Accused in the murder of his White ex-wife, and some other guy. It reeked of sex and slowly of race. Slowly, in fact, all the perfections fell away: The DNA wasn't perfect, the blood wasn't perfect, the timing was tight and then from left field the glove didn't fit.

Fast Food Delite provided an interesting view of America. The food, which was hamburger, attracted a universal clientele that transcended culture, race and economic status. It was on such a day that the White customers from a nearby office buildings came for their postponed lunch. It was the day after the Mark Furman tapes. Beyond being a good witness, which in this case he wasn't, Mark Furman was a cop, the inner-city kind who gets the job done. It was he who found the guilty glove behind OJ's house. It was he who found the matching glove at the victim's house. The victim, a vivacious blond beauty named Nicole Brown Simpson, estranged wife of OJ Simpson.

Muhammad never had much dealings with the cops, but he did grow up in the sixties. A clear memory of his childhood was his grandmother putting him out of the room as southern officers attacked throngs of people on TV. His grandmother called these people Colored. To his childish eyes they were only a lot of people making a fuss. He remembered when his Grandmother's house was burglarized and his brother Abe asked if she was going to call the cops...
"For What?" She asked.
Soon he began to hear words like Martin Luther King, Black Panther and Black Muslims. He noticed, back there in the sixties, that all cops were White. Yet, in his juvenile mind this was natural as all the criminals on TV were white: Bonnie and Clyde (As played by Beatty and Dunaway), Al Capone (Interpreted by Robert Stack) and Jessie James (By the magnificent Tyrone Power). So it was surprising that the ugly ones on the 5 o'clock news were Colored and the cops were White.

The New York Times that his Grandmother had so loved hadn't started calling Colored people Black yet, a term his Grandmother despised back in 1967. She though, along with everybody, fell into the 'Black is Beautiful' thing. Yet Grandmom to this day never says black and she don't trust cops. But she trusted Charlie.

The young Muhammad Charles Smith didn't know what to call these strangers he saw on TV at 5 o'clock.

He knew that they always seemed to be accompanied by a White cop. And one day when a Negro was shot dead on TV after beating his wife he would never forget his grandmother saying…"Now if that was a White man…"

Now thirty years later the lawyers for OJ Simpson found a recording and a witness to the fact that the prosecution's star witness, Mark Furman, had said the dreaded "N" word. To make matters worse Mr. Furman was White. There in the closing days of August, 1995 it was there for the world to see. "….. Nigger!……Nigger……nigger." Somehow this man OJ Simpson who had literally pulled himself up from his bootstraps and achieved the American dream, to be a movie star and to marry a White woman, had fallen prey to the American nightmare of race. Charlie didn't really care if OJ was guilty or not but time after time, example after example in this "Crime of the Century" the words of Muhammad's grandmother came back to him during this murder trial…"Now if that was a White man…"

Taking orders from his white clientele who had postponed their lunch to hear the latest details from the trial, Muhammad almost had a front row seat into the secret psyche of America. Before he could take her order Charlie heard the distress in the voice from the rear of the line.

"So what if he said nigger, he's still guilty and deserves the electric chair"

"Maggie you can't say that. California doesn't even have an electric chair."

*Anonymous*

"They got niggers."

A few in the restaurant gave Maggie the eye.

"Maggieeeee."

Muhammad continued taking orders. Then suddenly…

"SHE'S DEAD! Get over it mister. Just give me your order."

It was Tamika, the cashier on the other line. Muhammad just gave her the eye and took his next order…It was Maggie's turn.

"Welcome to Fast Food Delite, may I take your order?"

"Yes, I'll have a Double Delite with a large Orange soda and medium fries. No make that bigger…"

Tamika flew across the counter.

"Nigger!!! Who you callin' a Nigger ya White B…."

"TAMIKA!"

Muhammad had to be sharp. Tamika stopped but she seethed, staring at the now frightened White woman.

"Tamika, take your break."

"But Mr. Smith she said Nig…"

"Tamika! Take your break."

She stormed off.

"Why the nerve."

Maggie found her voice.

"Renee come up and take register two."

Turning promptly to his customer.

"Mam please accept your order as compliments of Fast Food Delite."

*The Adventures of Muhammad Smith and The Million Man March*

"Well, I never. I hope you're going to fire that young lady."

"Mam your order and your friend's order are on the house."

The bargain of free food seemed to satisfy her and lunch hour passed into a slow afternoon with Tamika still employed. But Charlie realized that no matter what the verdict White America was going to either be really glad or really mad. Black America…Well what did that matter.

It was a month earlier when the prosecution invited our Mr. OJ to put on the glove that was found behind his house by the dubious detective Mark Furman. The prosecution was smug, the defense surprised…The smoking gun lurked just inches away. From the small TV, hidden in the rear of the restaurant, Charlie swore he could see all of America holding it's breath as OJ was forced to place the proof of his own guilt onto his bloody hands. Once OJ put on that glove for all the world to see his fate would be sealed and the obvious would be verified. Charlie couldn't remember the last time he had put on a pair of gloves and they didn't fit. In a way so many gloves seem to fit so many hands…Fit like a glove. But once OJ puts on these gloves all of that would be forgotten and he was going direct to jail…Such a shame for one who had so achieved the American dream. That's not what the lunchtime Whites thought. They thought he should be hung from the nearest tree. His crime was despicable. A White Woman! Dead at the dirty hands of the wanton Negro. It's all the Whites talked about at lunch, it's all the Blacks talked about at dinner, it's all anybody was talking about.

*Anonymous*

The case would be slam shut as soon as OJ put on those gloves.

After much effort, on everyone's part...

...The gloves didn't fit!

The bloody gloves did not fit.
They were too small.
So strange.
So amazing.
The gloves did not fit.

But that was a month ago, today he was in charge of flipping burgers at Fast Food Delite. It was a nice Fast Food Delite in a nice neighborhood. Right on the northern edge of downtown Philly near Fairmont. The crowd was mostly White during lunch and after 4PM mostly Black. That's why Muhammad Charles Smith was the manager at that time. The owner was a third cousin, twice removed. His grandmother begged him the job after he was laid off from the telephone company. He detested working at some McDonalds joint but at the same time he needed money and at least he wasn't flippin' the burgers. His worthless associates degree gave him the minimum requirement for manager and he fit right in. He kept to task, directed the employees and smiled for the customers, especially the White customers and the occasional professional Black who crowded the lunch time hour but were nowhere to be found after 4PM, almost like OJ.

Dumping the fries from the cooker to the tray Muhammad wondered how well OJ would survive his first shower in jail. In Muhammad's mind OJ was guilty but it would be "cute" if he got off. That was his feeling from the get go. Even the first few hours after the crime had been committed and OJ had yet to be charged. Even when the news of murder flashed around the world, complete with one picture of this pretty, dead, White woman who was the wife of a Black man, even then Muhammad thought, 'be nice if he got off'. No rhyme, no reason just nice if he got off.

# Beginning of an Idea: RALPH CRAMDEN

Muhammad got his name because at the moment of his birth his mother was infatuated with a Black Muslim who had just got out of jail. Just like Malcolm she thought. But this Muslim guy wasn't Muhammad's father nor was he Malcolm X and before MC was circumcised this dude was gone.

It was the luck of the draw that something clicked when his grandmother taught him his ABC's, it tripped him into a chain of events that gave him the ability to read. Not the Daily News kind of reading but the New York Times kind. Still reading doesn't mean common sense. It doesn't mean you won't buy the most expensive car you see with your last dollar. Today Muhammad is driving a 10 year old Cadillac, working at a burger joint, waiting for the verdict of some rich guy and dreading the day his car note is due. Still he was doing better than his brother who was in jail.

*********

*The Adventures of Muhammad Smith and The Million Man March*

"My brother, my brother".

Maleek Rasheed walked in at 5:55PM complete with copies of "The Final Call" and two bean pies. If it wasn't a paper to sell, it was a donation to make if not that it was a bean pie to buy. Muslims, Black Muslims or the "Nation of Islam" always seemed to have a donation gimmick. For the longest it was a Hospital but today it was the Million Man March. Muhammad patronized Maleek as Maleek held a certain respect in the area after 4PM. This week's donation was for the 'First Annual Million Man March': A day of atonement.

"Yeah, yeah whatever Malik. Here's your dollar for your Million Man March"

The Million Man March, the Muslims had been littering telephone poles with signs about their day of atonement for weeks. Little more than an apology for Malcolm X Muhammad thought. Another gimmick, as the lofts of Malcolm X had long since been abandoned by the very Black men who had shot him dead. There was nothing new.

Race was nothing new in America, but California! Once the refuge of run-away slaves and now the epicenter of all that was bad. Rodney King beaten like a dog on international TV. Charlie wasn't sure which pissed him off more, the fact that Rodney was beaten or the fact that it took a video camera to prove it to him. Without the luck of a video camera Rodney King would only be another nigger crying foul on page seven of the local newspaper. It took a video camera to prove it to Muhammad. Did Muhammad need proof? This thought pissed him off as much as the beating.

Then, before Rodney King could beat up his next girlfriend, up pops OJ. An uppity Black man entwined as a White man who suddenly was being accused of being a Black man. Now Tamika, a struggling 20 year old single parent trying to make ends meet at community college as she earned pennies from Fast Food Delite, placing OJ above all else. There was something in the air across this American land that just wouldn't go away. But now it was time to go home.

In his car MC threw down the Muslim "Final Call" to the passenger seat. The rear page faced up with a picture of the honorable Minister and an advertisement for the Million Man March. OCTOBER 16, 1995. A thought slowly crept into Muhammad's mind. The most educated minds in America predicted the OJ trial would be over at the end of September. October 16th just might be in time for...

He drives, he's home, the phone rings. It was cousin James, the boss. Charlie followed an impulse.

"The Million Man March, are you going to the Million Man March?"

This isn't what the owner wanted to hear. James Johnson Brown was an established Black man who had the perfect wife, the perfect kids and in the perfect suburb. He called his day manager, a distant cousin, once or twice a week to get a feel for the restaurant to be sure everything was going ok. He owned four

*The Adventures of Muhammad Smith and The Million Man March*

Fast Food Delites and could care less about the latest Muslim gimmick.

"Charlie what are you talking about?"

"The Million Man March. Don't tell me you haven't heard about the Million Man March."

"Charlie, I call you to determine cash flow and since when are you so concerned about anything Black?"

"Cuz I got a feeling this is going to be big. I'm thinkin' Negroes will be so pissed after the OJ trial they'll flock to DC."

"You just refuse to call Black people Black don't you Charlie?"

"Last I checked James, the New York Times had us down as African American but that ain't the point. The point is the OJ trial is touching something James. It's touching something I want to tap."

"Charlie the Muslims got that whole thing tied up. Besides ain't no million niggers goin' to DC, that's probably part of the gimmick. How's the shop, any problems?"

"Million 'niggers'? Now there's the kettle calling the pot black. The shop is cool James, just that the lunch crowd is a tad dispersed with everyone watching the trial and all. 9 o'clock LA time is lunch hour for us and everyone wants to see every last bit of this trial. This is what I'm talking about James, there's an energy there that's got nowhere to go after the verdict except the Million Man March. Are you going? How can WE make some money?"

"WE can make money if you stop smoking that stuff and make sure all the workers get to work on time. How much were the receipts from your shift?"

"About 45 hundred."

*Anonymous*

"About? Excuse me Charlie but can you be more exact?"

Pulling a paper from his pocket Muhammad reads the exact figure.

"47 29 and 37 cents. If we can figure a way to tap into the two million Negroes going to DC that would be chump change James."

"Tell you what Muhammad, you let the Muslims manage DC and we'll manage the shop. OK?"

"OK cuz, ok."

"Say hi to Aunt Sally for me. Take care Charlie."

"Yeah sure man, take care."

With the click of the phone, Muhammad thought of one thing, himself. But now it was time for one of his all time favorite shows, "The Honeymooners". Muhammad lit a joint and turned the TV on.

"How was the job today Ralph?"

"The boss gave me the Harlem route today Alice, Harry called out sick."

"My uncle has a store on 125$^{th}$ Street"

"That's your Uncle Ben. Hey ain't he the one who sells the pig feet Alice. Pig feet HA! Who would of ever thought you could support a family on pig feet. Hey didn't you use to call him Uncle Ben the Pig Feet man."

Ralph, Jackie Gleason, swaggered a smile.

"That was before he brought the Cadillac and the house on Long Island."

"Alice that's it! I can make a fortune with a bus route from Harlem to the horse track out on Long

*The Adventures of Muhammad Smith and The Million Man March*

Island. Those folks in Harlem are always looking for a quick buck."

Alice gives him the eye.

"The folks in Harlem or the pig in Queens?"

"Ohhh youuu, I oughta…Wait a minute, Norton's got that old bus out in Jersey, If I could only…NORTON."

Just then it hit Muhammad like a ton of bricks. The buses were the key. The buses were the money maker. In Philly alone he could sell a package for thirty five dollars along with a bologna sandwich. He knew the routine from the bus trips that he organized on his job before he got laid off. All for the cause: The Black cause, the Malcolm cause or any cause they wanted to call it, it was perfect. Muhammad Charles Smith felt a buzz in the air. An opportunity that few would realize and most would not understand. Race had reared it's ugly head again and the feelings, as always, were strong. Such an event happens maybe once every ten years where the janitors and Doctors of a particular ethnic group get collectively pissed off. Sometimes it's an un-noticeable group like the Indians, Mexicans or Puerto Ricans. This time it was that once in fifty year event between Blacks and Whites. Not only was there a pretty White woman involved, but also an ex junkie who happened to be speeding on the wrong highway. Muhammad was sure that the friction between the stupid Rodney King and the tragic Nicole Simpson would generate anger and money. With each passing day the atmosphere would grow more charged with an intangible but palatable energy. A few short years ago ALL Blacks wanted to riot over the outrageous Rodney King verdict and White America was stunned that such anger could exist. Now there was OJ Simpson and White America was awaiting the justification of a verdict. There was a mistrust in the air almost as if Whites wanted to riot and Blacks only wanted to sit back and laugh. Yet in their laughter they were deemed stupid: To dumb to see that a guilty man was getting away. No one would use the words mistrust, laughter, stupid or dumb in public. Yet in all of this Muhammad saw one thing….Money.

There was a certain simplicity to it. Call the bus company, ask for prices, reserve the day. Most of these companies were mom and pop operations with fleets of only five or ten buses. They were plentiful throughout the region and much cheaper than the national chains, without the free video. It was much cheaper to go to DC for 35 bucks round trip rather than 55, one way, on Greyhound. Renting a 24-hour bus for two hundred and fifty dollars divided nicely over 40 paying customers doing their "patriotic" duty. The problem was credit and Muhammad's lack thereof. His current max was 5,892 dollars and 53 cents. This left him with 25 buses. Muhammad wanted more.

There was more to this OJ, Rodney, Muslim, Malcolm, Black, Race thing than met the eye and somehow Mr. Muhammad Charles Smith tripped up to where he could see it clearly.

Born as a child in a high rise, subsidized housing complex, Muhammad had seen desperation not only in the home he shared with his mother and his twin brother Abraham but he also saw desperation in the face of everyone he saw. Only the bused schooling he received by way of his reading skills allowed Muhammad a different view of the world. He saw White culture and it's belief of an orphanage for every orphan, perhaps even to include him. Was it his fault that he knew of a world where such perfection didn't exist? For Muhammad, from an early age he saw what he called the "Separation of American Cultures". For him this separation came down to one word: Perfection.

It was Muhammad's belief that Blacks and Colored People and Negroes and Afro-Americans and Nubians and African Americans would all want to go to the Million Man March. In all strata of Black society from the academic, the corner boy and the business man everyone would want to go. If someone controlled the buses they could grab a quick buck. It was a gamble, but a gamble that Muhammad was ready to take. Dreary from the marijuana he smoked Charlie slowly fell asleep…With no action and only a gamble for a plan, or a dream.

Waking the next morning his mind kicked into gear. With a new plan altogether. He had a plan, BUT he lived in an apartment and was still paying off his ten year Cadillac bill thanks to a loan he took out after the 60 month lease. At the last minute he chose the buy option. The closest thing he had to a real girlfriend often insisted on dinner at a downtown restaurant before he was allowed the full expression of his desires. And his HBO Cable bill was just enough to break the casual habit of buying music. He was broke and his five grand in credit wasn't going to cut it. There was only one place he could go for the kind of money he needed, family. And money meant one thing in his family, his cousin and boss James Johnson Brown. . The phone was the choice of contact.

"James, James, it's me Charlie…Good Morning."

"Charlie it's 6:30 in the morning. Why are you calling me at 6:30 in the morning Charlie?"

"I'm only returning your call, Cuz."

"Every time you say 'Cuz' I hear money Charlie. What do you want?"

"The Million Man March thing, I know how we can make a buck."

"Number one Muhammad, ain't no one going to the Million Man March. It ain't nothing but a gimmick. Number two who's gonna try to make money on the Fruit of Islam?"

James spoke the truth. Many mainstream Blacks ignored the Million Man March at the end of August 1995. Younger Blacks were only looking for a party.

"James, this OJ thing is going to be over soon, and White people are either going to be real glad that Negro got the chair or real mad if he get's off: After all the gloves didn't fit. James there's going to be an explosion of frustration, not anger, but frustration…After the OJ verdict that frustration is going straight to Washington DC James and I'm driving the bus."

"Muhammad what in the world are you talking about?"

"Lease four hundred buses at 250 per, and sell the seats for 40 bucks round trip. With a hundred grand I can get this thing going."

*The Adventures of Muhammad Smith and The Million Man March*

"Charlie, it's early in the morning, you're dreaming... No one is going to the Million Man March."

Ignoring what he was hearing Charlie continued.

"Look I can get 20 buses on my own, but I need a hundred grand to get four hundred buses."

"Four hundred buses, What are you talking about Charlie, there ain't even 400 Muslims going to the Million Man March, It's a Farakhan production and that's that. Hate to tell you this kid but you're dreaming again. Listen, whenever you want I'll sponser you to the Fast Food Corporate school in Oklahoma. You could rise up the ranks quick Charlie..."

"James I could put twenty buses in cities and college towns from Atlanta, Georgia to Syracuse, New York, charge 40 bucks a ride and make a clear grand off of each bus. Maybe some extra money for advertising and phone lines."

"Or a nickel bag Charlie."

"James, people are going to go to DC and they're going to pay me. Yeah it might be a gamble but I never felt more sure in my life."

"Well you can spare your breath Charlie because I'm not giving you a hundred thousand dollars or a diamond mine in Africa."

"Well that's pretty stro..."

"Charlie you haven't done anything since high school graduation. You always create these grand plans based on your intuition, which I admit can be accurate at times, but you DO nothing. Zip, zero, nada, never is there any action Charlie. So let's do us both a favor and finish our sleep, take our showers and go to work. I'll be down the shop today around twelve...Take care Charlie."

*Anonymous*

There was no need to wait for the click of the phone, this was how James was. Besides what could Charlie say to the truth. But just off the corner at Broad and Fairmount stood a fleet of mom and pop buses: Built for the long haul, but 15 years old and hand painted. They stood in the lot of the once famous and now demolished Center City Cadillac, when Cadillacs were king. With the phone still in his hand he grabbed a nearby phone book and flipping through it's yellow pages he found his mark: 'Fairmount Bus Company, 1339 Fairmount Ave…215-555-2625'.

"Hello is this Fairmount bus?"

\*\*\*\*\*\*\*\*

Within the hour he was at the Fairmont Bus Company. It was just around the corner from his burger joint. The building was little more than the worn out store front that he had expected, attached to a large lot full of buses, all four of them.

"Hello, is Mr. Appleby here, I spoke to him this morning concerning a rental in October."

The woman at the desk remained silent

"Yeah, here I is."

This voice came from the rear. From the rear appeared an old Black man with bib overalls, old dirty boots and carrying a wrench in his hands.

"So you one of the real folks?"

"Real folks Mr. Appleby?"

"Folks who actually shows up after a phone call. What can I do you outta young man. You's that Muhammad fella ain't ya?"

"Yes that would be me and you are Mr. Appleby?"

"In the flesh and here to serve. So you want a bus for October 16th. You got a driver?"

"I thought I made it clear that you would supply the driver."

"Yeah that was clear alright young fella, but I gave you the driverless price. With a driver that's gonna run ya three hundred dollars. You got $300 dollars young man?"

"Mr. Appleby our arrangement was for 250."

"That was til I saw how young you were. Don't need no hoodlums tearin' up my bus Mr. Muhammad and I'll need a fifty dollar deposit on the bus."

"So is the fifty for the driver or the deposit Mr. Appleby?"

"Both. Which brings our total to three hundred and fifty."

"350! Mr. Appleby you do know I can just go around the corner to Inner-City Motors"

"Yeah that would be my half brother Marvin. I'll call him and tell him you're comin'

His prices start at 400."

"That's not what he said this morning."

"That was before he saw some suit and tie businessman pop through his door. Oh he'll accommodate you just fine Mr. Muhammad."

Mr. Appleby turned to the young Muhammad and smiled with his one good gold tooth.

"We use to church folk Mr. Muhammad. You don't rightly sound like church folk. Is you church folk Mr. Muhammad?"

"My name is Muhammad Charles Smith. The Muhammad is from my mother not my religion. And if you must know I grew up in the AME church down on

*Anonymous*

Second Street and I'm the day manager at the Fast Food Delite around the corner. I was merely trying to give the neighborhood some business before I went downtown to some White Man. But seein' as how we all Niggers anyway Mr. Appleby, I'll just slide downtown and do the White folk shuffle.

"Hold on young fella, ain't no need for all that dancin' and carryin' on. I got your bus right here."

"The agreed upon 250 Mr. Appleby"

He pulled out three pieces of money.

"Or is Ben Franklin a Philadelphian you'd rather not see?"

The female Clerk looked to Mr. Appleby who stood looking at Muhammad.

"Well let me help you out with them dead Philadelphians Mr. Muhammad. I think we got ourselves a deal."

"No we don't have a deal. I want all four buses with a fifty dollar discount for a total of 950. That's the deal Mr. Appleby. It's the middle of the week, there ain't no school trips, no church trips and it's two days before welfare checks so there ain't no Casino trips. I'm the only game in town and that's my price Mr. Appleby."

The clerk stared at Appleby, eyes peeping over her tabloid paper. This time Appleby was quick.

"You got some more of them dead Ben Franklins Mr. Muhammad, or is that Mr. Smith?"

"Ten minutes to the bank."

"And twenty minutes to your buses Mr. Smith."

With a handshake MC had his first buses, only three hundred and ninety six more to go.

Before work that Thursday Muhammad had taken a first step not only towards his plan but for his ego. There had to be more to life than shuffling workers from the fry machine to the griller. There were two more days to this week, his work week. He collected the names of Bus companies. Bargaining for prices and insisting on a contract to insure rental. By time Saturday came he had the lease for the 25 buses he could afford.

By the end of Saturday Charlie had gone through his credit card and had his twenty five buses. He was flat broke but felt that an investment had been made and that he was on his way. He realized that his suit and tie routine was a help with the White bus companies but with the Black mom and pops the suit and tie seemed to put them off. It didn't put Charlie off. He had a plan now and he was on task. He had 25 buses and a tapped out credit card. All he needed now was a bunch of Negroes willing to pay the way. Muhammad Charles Smith: Negro Extraordinaire.

# The Plan: DETAILS AT ELEVEN

MC, Charlie, Muhammad or Mr. Smith it didn't matter to Muhammad Charles Smith. His grandmother insisted on Charlie for her own reasons while most of his family floated between Charlie and Muhammad. As a youngster on the dark ghetto streets of North Philly 'Muhammad' was the nom de jour. In his bused Chestnut Hill schools full of Whites 'Charles' worked just fine. Sometimes he would laugh when his fellow students would ask what was the 'M' for of M. Charles Smith. A secret he would never tell. He could never forget how a friend at an earlier school so turned on him upon the discovery that this little Black boy carried the name of Muhammad. Perhaps this was the same pride in which MC insisted on being called a Negro.

For him it was rhythmic, soothing and almost even French. Plus he so loved to see Whites almost say Nigger: A certain thrill he had cultured throughout his life. Yet it all began when his mother and a current 'uncle' had a huge argument over weather he should call himself Nubian or Afro-American. His mother so loved Afro-American with it's heritage. While her boyfriend of the moment felt that Nubian carried a certain unity. Utterly confused, young Muhammad looked in the dictionary and couldn't find either word and then for some reason he looked up the word NEGRO:

> A member of a race of humankind derived from Africa. (also see Negroid).

For him this was a magic he couldn't explain. And as the names came and went, often depending on the prerogative of the New York Times; Colored, Black, African-American and the all time favorite, Nigger, MC always stuck with Negro.

But all that and 50 cent left him flat broke with little more than 25 buses, no passengers and a rich cousin who might come through. He sat in his apartment looking at HBO wondering how money could grow on trees. Watchin' burgers flip at Fast Food Delite wasn't gonna' cut it. Still he had to go to work on Monday. His next check was already spoken for in the person of a ten year old Cadillac note and the very HBO that he was watching. The culmination of his financial expertise to this point in his life. What the heck, even with the 25 buses he figured on making 25 grand, more if he sold the bologna sandwiches. Maybe the brothers might even want to spring for a shot of vodka. Ideas were plenty, yet it all depended if his hunch was right that the OJ verdict along with a growing White anger and the bitter memories of Rodney King would lead the Negroes, he so loved, to the fiery speech of the Honorable Louis Farakhan.

RINGGGG, RINGGGG.

No one called Charlie at this time of night even though it was only eleven and the Action News jingle was preparing to report the murder of the day here in his city of brotherly love. What he called a girlfriend was either in bed with him sleeping at this time of night or home alone. His small circle of friends had evaporated since he was laid off and the few people he laughed with at Fast Food Delite didn't even know his real name much less his phone number.

RINGGGG, RINGGGG.

In fact usually his phone was off at this time of night but tonight it was on perhaps hoping to get a call from James. But why be humiliated again.

RINGGGG, RINGGGG.

'Perhaps after four rings they'll go away' but, true to the discipline of his life, that's the very moment he answered it.

"Hello?"

"Charlie"

"Grandmom?, Why are you were up at 11PM"

"I've been thinking about you Charlie. Isn't that good enough reason to watch Action News?"

The sound of the Action News jingle created a stereo effect as it flowed though both of their phones.

"What do you think grandmom, I'm going to be the murder of the day or you want to talk about the weather?"

Their love was real.

"James called me today Charlie and he told me about your hairbrained scheme: Four hundred buses to Washington DC. Is that prudent Charlie?"

"If I get buses in several cities up and down the coast, yeah I think there could be a market."

"Why?"

"In the shop this week I saw the energy grandmom. The energy from the Blacks and the Whites and more important grandmom I saw the emotions when these people were crowded into one room. This OJ thing is gonna blow up grandmom. When that Jury comes back with their verdict sometime in September Whites are going to blow up. Now excuse my French grandmom but they're either going to blow a load or they're going to blow a fit. Either way Negroes are going to need a response. That response grandmom is going to be the Million Man March. The memory of Rodney King is so fresh. In everybody's voice I hear such passion, excitement and anger. It's there grandmom, I know it is. It's there for the taking. I already got 25 buses, reserved and paid for. I figure with 40 seats to a bus and 35, 40 dollars a seat that's a thousand dollars profit for each bus. It's right there Grandmom."

"I haven't heard you this excited since you did the science project on water."

"So you see this as one of my childish adventures grandmom?"

"James says you asked him for 100,000 dollars. Why so much?"

"Grandmom I want all the buses from Philly to Pittsburg and from Boston to Atlanta. You know Grandmom, I know it sounds like a gamble but all I got after 37 years of life is a broken down Cadillac..."

"And now you want a bus?"

"Grandmom, I don't mean to be rude but it's been a long da..."

*Anonymous*

"I will give you the 100,000 dollars Charlie."

"What did you say?"

"I will give you the 100,000 dollars."

She spoke with a sudden clarity that told Charlie this was no joke, but it was still a gamble.

"First of all Grandmom, I don't believe you got that kind of money. Second of all even if you did have that kind of money I wouldn't take it. If the least little thing went wrong the whole family would treat me like they treat my mom. Plus I could never look you in the eye again. Naw, this is my gamble."

"Charlie If you're not here at 7 o'clock tomorrow night I will think you a fool and I will never forgive you for it. Be here tomorrow Charlie."

"Listen Grandmom, thanks but…"

"Charlie do you remember you got an "A" for that water science project and they put you on the 11 o'clock news that night and I let you stay up late to watch it?"

Sometimes there is no answer to love. Only silence can speak of it's gratitude and integrity."

"Yeah but you gave me the water Grandmom."

"7 o'clock tomorrow young man."

As she was prone to do she let her actions speak the final word and she hung up on him. Ain't love grand.

********

Grandmom's second husband, Jay Livingston, was a successful man with a bar near 15$^{th}$ & Girard. He was sharp in mind and dress. Uncle Jay was the first to introduce MC to the joy of a Cadillac. It was a maroon Eldorado, with a black vinyl top: Fading from contemporary style but so alluring in his memory.

Yeah that was Uncle Jay, a quick joke and then off to his corner quietly watching everything. As if all was under his control. Yeah he was cool until he got shot in the eye back in '68. It was the typical shooting, Black on Black. It never did make the paper, but he was dead all the same.

Fact is Mr. Jay Livingston, somewhere along the course of his calm and jokeful life, had picked up the habit of buying life insurance policies. He very often let them expire, yet just as often he could have seven, eight or even ten policies in effect at any given time. When he died he had eleven. Nothing massive mind you but when Uncle Jay got shot in the eye and died three days later, he quietly left Grandmom 250,000 1968 dollars. Sometimes grandmom claimed MC's mother was Jay's child. But everyone knew the girl was Charlie's kid, old Charlie, grandmom's first husband. But all that "his kid, my kid" stuff faded away when grandmom was the only one standing with a lot of dough. Grandmom went through a few men but grandmom had a certain sense. She brought a few houses in Germantown, two in West Philly, the Wynnfield section and the one she lived in, in South Philly at 9$^{th}$ and Christian Streets. Today she was a retired teacher with a pension, but we always wondered where she got her money.

There were certain restrictions to Grandmom's money. She signed all checks. This was not a blank check for Charlie to make Cadillac payments. Grandmom Sally wanted a receipt for everything. She was open to extras like posters for advertising, but no Cadillac payments. After one week MC had reserved, with cash and contract, two hundred buses in the city for October the 16th, 1995. Now it was time for a decision. He had already decided that he was going across the river to Camden, NJ, the real decision was to leave Fast Food Delite.

The past week was full of packed mornings, rushing to be at work by 10AM and weary nights because after six, there was still work to be done. He needed the day, not only to stay to task but also to organize just a bit better than he had been. In spite of grandmom's generosity he held it as a point of discipline not to use the money for anything else except the buses and then there was that small matter of pride. Still he was hungry and his girlfriend kept dropping hints that her birthday was coming up and she expected more than last year's trip to Great Adventure. It was frustrating in a way that builds character. He had access to a hundred grand and 200 buses but he was living on a check from Fast Food Delite. Then there was Stevie from 63rd Street, near Market.

Stevie was thought to be the child of Jay Livingston, which is how Charlie got to know him. Not that they were friends, Charlie and Steve, but he was around just enough for Charlie to call him cousin. Stevie didn't go the High School diploma route. He was a product of the streets and what little business savvy he picked up from his father he applied to the street. This is one reason he didn't quite fit in with what Grandmom considered a family and why he was raised by his own mother in North Philly. Today Stevie ran 63rd and Market. All the reefer that was sold on that corner ran through him, and that was a lot of reefer. He held the distinction of having the best weed on one of the most vibrant corners in Negro Philadelphia. Stevie loved the fact that he was on a first name basis with several of the cops who patrolled the area. His clothes came from Boyds of downtown Philly, his several cars included a Beamer which was his favorite on the sometimes narrow streets of inner-city Philadelphia. His hustles were many, reefer was just a foundation for coke, crack, the loan sharking and the whore house on Arch Street. A loan 'til payday to pay off a bill, buy some crack or even some money to buy a prostitute. It didn't matter as long as you paid back with the money on top. Stevie had no problems with breaking a leg or two for the money on top. There was always someone near 63rd Street with crutches. In fact 63rd and Market was known as Crutch-Town:

"Down on Crutch. You know when you see the nigger with the crutches." was a popular refrain.

\*\*\*\*\*\*\*\*

She was White. Deep and dark Italian White, but none the less she was White and the girlfriend of Muhammad Charles Smith. Perhaps a reflection of Muhammad's world. For his grandmother such worlds did not exist. And even as his grandmother straightened her hair and avoided the sun for fear that it would make her darker, she still hated White people. But no grandmother was going to keep Muhammad from this White woman. He met Carmillia at Community College on Spring Garden Street. It was math class and 'Carm', as he had come to know her, was struggling with Algebra. From the drills James forced him through as a child in grade school Muhammad knew math well.

And as soon as Carmillia asked for the answer to one and one, MC knew the answer.

She wasn't Charlie's first White girl. Charlie had been doing white girls since he started the Chestnut Hill schools. He would never tell it but for Charlie White women held a certain purity enhanced by their European culture, white skin and silky hair. In those 'certain' situations with White women he loved the feel of a White woman melting in his arms. He could never imagine such a joy with a Black woman.

Now they were at Stetson's near $2^{nd}$ and Chestnut. They were regulars at this cosmopolitan watering hole where the bartenders knew their names, knew their drinks and knew the routine.

"Hey Carm, Chuckie…Long time no see. Whasss up?

"Just the routine Margaritas Tom."

"You tryin to call my Margaritas routine Chuckie?"

"I'll tell you what ain't routine Tom, the prices at this place. Six bucks for a drink."

"Don't you love it, the atmosphere, the people."

"Not like the atmosphere in Carm's bed."

Carmillia slapped his forearm. MC smiled. But the bartender's smiling lips quickly gave way to an eye of contempt.

"Yeah how bout that Chuckie."

Charlie turned his attentions back to Carmillia.

"So Miss Carmillia when's the best time I can breathe in some atmosphere."

She slapped his arm again but this time leaned over to his ear.

"For that I get one bite."

*The Adventures of Muhammad Smith and The Million Man March*

"Will it be hard?"

Drinking her fresh Margarita she smiled, he smiled and the bartender took the next drink.

"So how's the job hunt."

"I'm not really looking right now Carm. I think I got something better."

"Well anything is better than flipping burgers at ten bucks an hour."

"It's thirteen bucks and yes anything is better than flipping burgers."

"Honey, I don't want to talk business, I want to go home."

"But we just got here."

"Please?"

He smiles, she sips her drink and then kisses him.

"Is that what you tell all the boys?"

She whispers in his ear.

"Only the big ones."

Pulling her face away their cheeks rub, cheek to cheek. He turns for a kiss, a soft kiss, direct and hot with a nibble.

"You don't really want to stay, do you?"

"…Hey man, here's your tip. I see you later."

"Yeah, later dude."

She makes her way quaintly to the door and holds it for him and smiles as he approaches. Her arm finds it's embrace around his waist. He reciprocates with an arm across her shoulder. They walk so close. Soon there is the doorman at the massive Walnut Towers Apartments and Condominiums. He holds the door for the two lovers.

"Good Evening Mam"

"Hello William"

She smiles as if in victory leading the way through the door and to the elevator. She so loves her Sunday nights.

Chuckie enters the elevator and barely presses the button to the floor he knows so well when he feels her behind him. But more important, she feels him. She is in rare form. He turns, grabbing her arms and then looks into her eyes. He means to give her what she wants.

Kissing her he pulls her to him where her arms can embrace a juicy treat: Feeling all that is solid about him. He holds her tighter as her soft body reveals a thirst for desire. Without knowing it her back is against the elevator wall where she can suddenly feel the full extent of his intentions.

'DING'

This is where they get off.

Politely they walk down the hall to her apartment. Once at her door his arm leans on the frame. She feels his breath and calmly opens her door. Walking into the darkness the hall light slices into the room but Chuckie takes the knob and then her, by the waist. The door is closed. It's now the two of them alone in the dark.

He presses her to the door. She turns to greet him with open arms. And they kiss. From its very inception the kiss is warm, strong and wet. Only the power of their hips betray them. Their arms caress as their lips now press wildly, still second to the emotion between their thighs. Then she bites him, on the neck, and he gives the appropriate moan. Taking no more temptation, his extended hands suddenly push from behind. But she pushes him away, to the floor.

Now only their clothes remain, but soon even that was no obstacle. They lay in each other's arms with only a tidal wave of heat, passion and hormones to hold their full and complete attention. As if a machine, the excitement held a certain rhythm to the beat of his body slamming into hers. Right there on her shampooed white carpet. There was no need to stop now. That taste of sin, a bite here or a nibble there. As tongue met skin there would be no secret hiding place upon the shampooed white carpet.

It was Sunday night, sex night. An almost weekly ritual with MC and Carmillia that he, they enjoyed since Community College, five years ago. After one homework assignment for a Monday morning class the game was on and the assignment had been Carmillia's apartment ever since. There were other boyfriends and girlfriends but the two of them seemed to always make their Sunday nights. They knew their place. For her it was a Mandingo thing, so much so that she put the word out of her mind. For him the attraction was strong. To run his fingers through her hair, her long silky hair and when she did the honky whip….Intoxication is not too strong of a word.

It was 1995 and Muhammad had the last of the Jerry Curls. Hair chemically treated to a shine and brushed into a patch of greasy curls. Above this he had the whitest teeth possible. It wasn't a testament to dental hygiene but more a reflection of his lifestyle. Sting was his poet and entertainer of the moment. Luther Vandross was a non-entity. In the humor of Jerry Seinfeld he saw great psychological insights: Yada, yada, yada. In Chris Rock he saw a Black dude cryin' cause he was Black. Chuckie swore that if he heard "Now if that was a Black man..." one more time. It seemed to be the common punch line for every Negro comedian since Richard Pryor. But holding Carmillia in his arms there on her couch, this was the lifestyle that he wanted. Not the Black world of Stevie and Stephanie Morgan.

# Life as usual: PEYTON PLACE

Stephanie Morgan was a Black Woman, or as she currently preferred, African American. But Black Woman was just as good. She was one of seven Blacks who made the trip to the schools of Chestnut Hill with Muhammad when they were children. As MC grew to enjoy and embrace White culture, Stephanie loathed it. Her's was the world of North Philly, which in Philadelphia was slang for the Black neighborhood. Stephanie's parents wore Dashikis, the African dress of the day and her grandparents hated White people.

Yes, she was educated in the fine White schools where she was bused to, but with her education she created I.S.I.S., an acronym for the Egyptian goddess that she named for the Inner-city Society for the Improvement of Sisterhood. It was 1995 but she still managed to parlay the White guilt of charitable organizations to finance her dream of Black pride. She was the last Black woman that Muhammad Charles Smith ever loved. It was in their youth, when they were high school students, he enjoyed his first sex while she admired a "Black man with a brain".

When she got pregnant just before high school graduation, MC quickly got a job with the city as a technical apprentice. But it was not to be. Stephanie's baby proved to be a stranger.

It was Charlie's grandmother who insisted on the blood test.

In those days it was far from exact. While it could prove that you were definitely not the father, it couldn't prove that you definitely were the father. The test came back negative: Charlie was not the father.

While he abandoned his college plans to support her and his planned family, Charlie's grandmother used every gimmick to separate them. Stephanie could only cry with her only defense being "It was only one time...Please don't leave me Muhammad." After the blood test he left her taking his city job and South Philly apartment with him.

The child, a boy, grew up looking more and more like Stevie Livingston. The only connection MC could ever make was the one time he caught her and Stevie sharing a laugh together.

Charlie had written her poetry, brought her flowers and often even opened the door. She finally opened up when she read his report on Martin Luther King during Black History month. Somehow she fell for the line "Without a culture of our own beyond the nuclear, biological and chemical pollution of this modern world we are forever condemned to second class citizenship". As a child he chased her with every hormone at his disposal as he could not imagine any other woman in his world to satisfy his hidden fantasies. He had no idea that she only saw him as a perfect mate, devoid of a passion that she didn't even know existed. Yet one chance meeting with a supposed juvenile delinquent cousin and she would discover passion, far more than once.

This baby was now approaching the age of 20 and went to the University of Pennsylvania, pre-med. Stephanie had raised him, Raheem Muhammad Morgan, as a single parent and did everything in her power so that he would not be the Oreo she had come to see in Muhammad. Knowing all this MC walked through the front door of I.S.I.S., the organization that Stephanie had created on the 7$^{th}$ floor at 12$^{th}$ and Chestnut Streets. There was Miss. Harris, an old lady who sat at the front desk and knew Charlie well.

"Well hello stranger. I ain't seen you in a good while. How you been?

"I'm fine Miss Harris. How are you?"

"Oh you know me Mr. Smith, just gettin' old. You looking for Stephanie?"

"Yes, as a matter of fact I am."

"She right back there in her office. You can go on back."

The office was in a short hallway just to the rear of Miss Harris. Muhammad made his way back to a door left partially open. He knocked.

"Who is it?"

"It's me Steph, Muhammad."

There was a noticeable pause…

"Come in."

"Hello Stephanie."

She was typing at the PC, writing yet another flyer for yet another trip to Washington or Harrisburg.

"What do you want Muhammad, or is it Chuckie today?"

He could only feign a smile.

"Can I move these papers to the side?"

"Yeah, set them right there."

Bypassing his eyes she pointed to a corner in her crowded office and then returned to her typing.

"What do you want my North American brother?"

"Been to Africa lately Steph."

He returned her jibe and she turned to him.

"You couldn't find Africa on a map."

"Is that what happened to us Stephanie, Africa."

"What do you want Muhammad?"

"Well to be direct I'm looking for Stevie. You seen him?"

"Come on brother, you know the line 'Do I look like his mother?'"

"You seen Stevie Steph? I need to see him."

"I can't remember the last time I seen him."

Exasperated she turns to him

"What a fine Negro like you want with a Black man like Stevie."

"I bump into him from time to time, but I need to see him now."

She turns back to the PC and a small pad she writes to and from.

"You still smokin' weed Muhammad?"

"Let's rise above that Stephanie. You know I wouldn't be here if I didn't have…"

With a frozen stare at her PC she interrupts his sentence…

"That's the problem Muhammad, you never have a reason to come by…"

The few times they spoke over the years they never mentioned the pregnancy or the blood test. So she rambled on about his shortcomings. In the end though she told him where to find Stevie.

With Stephanie behind him he made a quick run to Camden, to Cooper Blvd and reserved a fleet of buses with contract. The owner had no clue why this man wanted to rent all of his 39 buses in October, a slow time of year. But the owner of the buses was in it for himself and if this idiot was gonna rent out his fleet then he was perfectly happy to sign a contract that simply said the deal could not be canceled, which was a no-brainer. Muhammad Charles Smith had his contract.

After a long eight hours at Fast Food Delite, it was time to find Stevie and get some money. He made his way to the Havana Club on the East side of South Street. Stephanie told him Stevie was always here on Monday nights between 9 and 11. It was Margarita night. Margaritas were half price and it seemed that every so-called "Buppie" Negro in Philadelphia made it the place to be on Monday night. It was 1995 and there were still some who called themselves "Buppie". But nobody is racist, at least not in America.

As soon as Stephanie said it MC could of kicked himself for not knowing this was a natural place for Stevie to be. He always liked to hob-nob with the "Black Bourgeois" and Muhammad use to come here on a semi regular basis himself, but never on Monday. Muhammad never did like Buppies. But he was here tonight, in the thick of them. There were the females,

*Anonymous*

their hair permed right to the edge of the infamous honky whip (If only it were possible). Then there were the ones trying out the new weaves and braids. His mind flashed to Stephanie. She never did the Perm/Braid thing.

Then there were the other Buppies, the "Brothers". They were rough and manicured at the same time. Muhammad never got the manicured thing. He mismatched colors at will, almost on purpose, and white socks were his favorite. When he did wear sneakers he only wore canvas Converse, Chuck Taylor sneakers. The same 'bo-bo' style from 1965. In fact if he had any style at all it was from the Hippie wannabe days of his youth.

So there he stood with an old, gray and slightly oversized blazer over a hooded sweatshirt. His pants were plain Khaki and today he was wearing sneakers and a Jerry Curl. Leaning lightly on the wall he slowly drank his beer, waiting for cousin Stevie, when from the next room of the three room bar he heard…

"My Man!"

And then there was a loud clap.

"What's up baby?"

That voice, that confidence, that was Stevie. Muhammad turned to the room to see Stevie going through his barroom greetings.

"Hey Stevie, slide me some of that good stuff brother."

"Good stuff? You the man baby."

Then from the first bar…"

"What's up Stevie. Where you been?"

"Just gettin' by my brother"

*The Adventures of Muhammad Smith and The Million Man March*

The Havana was the kinda of place where you could call White people brother and the other Blacks present wouldn't be concerned. But still Whites couldn't call Stevie a Nigger even if he did wear a Jerry Curl. Stevie made his way through the cosmopolitan crowd. If not the best dressed cat in the place, he was the loudest. Muhammad just looked waiting for Mr. Stevie 'Wonder' to notice him. Which of course he did.

"You no dressin Negro from Miss Sally's house. What's up Charlie?"

"Thank you very much. I'll take that as a compliment."

"What you doin' down here? Lookin' for some smoke? You know I got the killer."

"I'm trying to keep busy. You know, be a good boy. How do you feel Mr. Stevie?"

"You know me Charlie, I just keeping it down. Keepin' it on the down low. Ain't nothin to it.

Then with a swagger...

"It's just a thang my brother."

Stevie glanced a laugh, Muhammad smiled.

"Hey Mikey, A margarita...No salt..." For Stevie it was all a party. "So my nigger, what you know good? You lookin' for some weed?"

"I saw Stephanie today. She s..."

Stevie's complete attitude changed like that.

"How Raheem? What's Raheem doin' these days?"

"You know he's doin' the Penn thing...That's kinda of big."

"Big! Nigger take after me."

They were quiet for a while.

"The only way I'm takin weed is if you givin' it away for free. And we know better than that."

"So straight up Charlie, why we here?"

"I need some money Stevie."

"For what? Them buses you been rentin' all over town? For that 'Million Man Thing'?"

"As a matter of fact Stevie, yes, that Million Man Thing."

"Ain't that a Farrakhan hook-up?"

"That would be his name Stevie, Louis Farrakhan."

"Humph."

"How you know about my buses?"

"Philly ain't as big as people think."

"I'll drink to that."

With a smile Charlie took a swig.

"So Charlie when you say money I know a nigger like you don't need a 100 bucks."

"Two grand Stevie, that's all I need to make it to pay day."

"That's a big pay day my brother."

"It's a jungle out there my brother."

"I'll drink to that."

From there it was all talk about Baseball, missed adventures and vague victories. It seemed that the Phillies weren't going nowhere and that was just fine with them. It had been a long time for these two.

"Naw man, I never saw her again."

"That was fun."

The night was over but Stevie insisted on "driving around the block". From the glove compartment he pulled out a decent bag of weed, the spicy green kind.

"Roll me up nigger."

He lifted the armrest to reveal a paper bag with Top Paper, another bag of weed, a nickel plated gun and money, lots of money. Stevie always was a show off. Soon they were driving down the comparatively dark Lombard Street smoking as if it were 1979.

"Charlie I think you on to somethin'. I even hear junkies talkin' 'bout the Million Man March. A matter of fact I heard Stevie Wonder on WDAS FM talkin' that 'All for one, One for all' junk. But you know little Stevie blind man is cool."

"Long Live Little Stevie Wonder. The biggest poet I know"

"Her love is Heavenly, when her arms enfold me, I hear a tender rhapsody, but in reality she doesn't even know meeee…Just my 'magination, runn…"

"Stevie that ain't Stevie Wonder."

"It ain't!?"

"That's the Delphonics"

"Delphonics my butt, that's Stevie wonder."

"If that's Stevie Wonder then I'm Ray Charles."

"Hey Charlie remember when me, you and Abe, use to come down here sneakin' into the clubs after school."

"Me, you and Abe. Ha! There's a laugh. I remember when Abe grabbed that Jeep on 3rd street…'It was just for fun' he said."

"Abe was one crazy nigger, I mean I know he was your brother and all but that nigger was crazy. Remember when that boy bumped into him down on Girard. He went off on that nigger. That's how I can tell yall apart from that scar on his lip."

*Anonymous*

"He like's it."

"So how many more years he got to go?"

"Five, maybe ten."

"Humph…Hey, hey, hey man pull out some of that money"

Charlie pulled out some paper from the bag to see a few wads of money, rolled up into rubber bands.

"The one with the 20 on top, grab that one. Come on, come on hurry up."

He takes a drag off the joint.

"Don't want nobody seein' my stuff. You grab that 20 roll, that's your stuff."

"Steve, what's a '20 roll'?"

"A 20 roll, that's old time lingo for 25 yards, you remember that don't you"

"You got 2,500 dollars in this little roll right here"

"You can have the 500 with no interest, but on the two grand you cracked for I want 20% in a month. Deal?"

"Deal"

"Alright put the rest of the cash in the bag and go buy some buses for your 'Million Man Thang'"

Stevie had driven him right to his Cadillac. With a handshake Charlie stepped out to his car but before he could close Stevie's car door, Stevie called him.

"Hey, hey Muhammad Charles…"

Charlie turned to see the bag of smoke on the car seat he had just left.

"Take your stuff man."

With a quick stare of hesitation Charlie grabbed the bag. A pocket of money, a bag of smoke and a ten year old Cadillac. All the elements of failure he thought. What a friend that Stevie.

Stevie would leave Center City and drive on to his home on 57th Street, maybe a mile from City Line Avenue. It would of been quicker to take the Schukill Expressway but Stevie always drove by 63rd and Market every chance he got. Market was five or ten miles from City Line Avenue. The distance didn't matter, 63rd and Market was his domain, his kingdom. His daddy would have been proud. The hacks were payin' him a cut and the drugs on this corner came mainly from him. He was a few layers removed from the street and the corner boys he now watched had no idea they were workin' for him. He turned the corner and drove by twice which is when the cop saw him. Up went the flashers, red and blue lights twirling around. Without hesitation Stevie knew he wanted to dump the gun. He was banned from owning a gun since he hit one of his ex-girlfriends…The law.

As if in one movement he grabbed the bag from the armrest and tossed it out the car through a chassis door in front of his seat. The cop didn't see it but the youngest of the corner boys saw the bag suddenly appear on the street as Stevie and the cop pulled over half a block away. The corner boy picked up the paper bag and was instantly impressed by it's weight. He ran on to the curb, looking at the bag. He found the gun and suddenly didn't notice the weed that fell to the ground. He found the money and a gun, the youngest of all the corner boys now had a gun.

Even though he took his time pulling over, the cop only held Stevie for 20 minutes as he scanned his license, registration and insurance. Stevie could only look in his rear view mirror as the young boy stuck the gun in his jacket and ran off. All he could do was turn on the music and wait: WDAS FM, as always, on a Motown Monday.

********

It was one of the rare times that Charlie listened to WDAS, he was really a KYW news man. Tonight though, it was Motown Monday…So what the heck. It was only weed. MC had often seen it as less dangerous than Jack Daniel's Kentucky Bourbon. In fleeting moments MC saw weed as a very definition of "Black" in America: Illegal but common. Almost just like Rap music had become, and like Little Richard's rock and roll had been, prancing around proclaiming itself to be King. Dodging from cops until it finally dawned on you that the cops didn't care. That could be good and bad, the cops not caring.

He threw the bag to the table as 'DAS played classics by Marvin Gaye. He remembered stories of Marvin and Diana recording together with Marvin insistent on smoking a joint. But Marvin was dead and Diana was married to her fourth husband, a rich guy out of Europe. Diana was always good at that and Marvin was dead. Later that night during a replay of the 11 o'clock news, Charlie pulled out a pack of Tops but only managed to throw them next to the bag of weed. Muhammad was unsure of tomorrow but once the bag and Tops were on the table they would stay there for the night. If tomorrow were to bring anything it would have to be beyond the stagnant joy of a joint.

# Perfect Timing: PERRY MASON

A week had passed and Mark Furman had pleaded the fifth, it stemmed from the minor use of the word 'Nigger' and other statements he had made under oath. Far removed from OJ's guilt the Furman thing took on a life of it's own and within a day the Appellate court had weighed in on the matter. Again, far from the matter of OJ's guilt. It was all but over, the prosecution had presented their case and the defense had rested. Still the case dragged on throughout the month of September. Already Muhammad's gamble had taken a wrong turn. He had hoped the trial would be over by the end of September and he could start selling seats on all these buses. It was the 28$^{th}$ and still they were questioning witnesses. MC had just distributed his advertising posters to be stapled onto telephone polls from Trenton to Wilmington. It was the last of his money. If something didn't happen soon he would have to sell his free lunches from Fast Food Delite. It was little solace when on the next day, a Friday no less, the jury finally got the case. They would probably take at least a week to decide, leaving little more than a week for the mass of Black America to decide, plan and go to the Million Man March even if they wanted to go. Would a week be enough time to make such a decision and plans. Muhammad had a sneaking suspicion that it would not be. And as the long weekend evolved Muhammad wondered how he would tell his grandmother that yet another of his grand schemes had fallen apart.

Monday came with a bang.

The Jury, the jury. Once, maybe six months ago, they were mad, collectively mad. The issue? OJ? No. The issue was that the routine guards had been removed, transferred, taken away and the jury was pissed, collectively pissed. The public barely noticed. The media saw it as a joke, but they all overlooked the word "collectively". On March 3$^{rd}$, 1995 the entire jury came to court collectively dressed in Black.

This jury, the OJ jury, was given the case on Friday, September 29$^{th}$. A long weekend but an even longer deliberation. How could it not be a long deliberation. To merely scan over the evidence from the past year would have taken a week or two. Of course throughout the weekend, that Saturday and Sunday, the talk was of nothing but the "All Star in Rent-A-Car", the Heismen Trophy winner, the star of screen, Monday Morning Quarterback Supreme who now stood accused of murder. The talk was of nothing else.

It was like any other early Monday afternoon except that America and the world were doing what they had been doing for the past year: Watching the TV screen

*The Adventures of Muhammad Smith and The Million Man March*

for the final word on one of it's greatest creations, OJ Simpson. How could it of come to an end so soon?

"Ahhhhh!!!!!!! AGGHHHhhhhhh!!!!!! A verdict! They reached a verdict!!!"

Only Tamika was in the rear with the secret TV. She was loud, but never like this.

"They done found that man guilty. I know it. That was q…"

"Tamika, what are you talking about?"

Charlie spoke but both he and the scattering of customers in the store looked for more. Charlie turned back to the customer, a stranger, who awaited every word from Tamika's mouth.

"The jury reached a verdict Mr Smith, that was fast. What they done done to that man."

There was a small sadness in her voice. The customers, strangers all, couldn't help but comment to the utter surprise of it all, and then…

"Well God bless Jesus. Justice has survived in America."

It was a customer, a stranger.

********

It had been a tough run for justice in America in 1995. A few years earlier Rodney King had found a place in textbooks across America when a video camera caught his municipal beating. The verdict on that case, where the cops got off against the evidence of video tape, caught America off guard. To this day no one really wants to speak of the spontaneous riots that broke out in several cities across the USA. It was that rare moment of Negro unity or maybe it was just anger. Whatever it was Black Doctors, Black janitors and even Grandmom, who went to church every Sunday, wanted to throw a brick at anything White. Muhammad never told his "Chuckie" friends but when Ronald Dennisen, a White man, a quite nice White man, was getting his brains banged out on National TV, Muhammad almost jumped for joy.

It was all an eye for an eye. A day or two after the riots had begun Muhammad was on Spring Garden Street at 9th Street near the Theopolis Gun Shop, the only gun shop Charlie had ever known of. In all this time, on this route to his grandmother's house, he had never noticed a crowd of people at the Theopolis gun shop before today. Today he saw three men going to the gun shop at the same time, three white men. The atmosphere was fully charged when those cops got off and Negroes threw a fit.

Then with practiced words so illiterately delivered yet so full of desperation and integrity:

"Can't we all just get along?"

Delivered by Rodney King.

The riots stopped.

And then shortly thereafter there was Susan Smith, the almost hilarious Susan Smith. A white woman from the trailers of Alabama who intentionally kills her kids by drowning them and claiming a Black Man did it. All so she could be alone with her boyfriend. Within hours there was an all points bulletin across several

*The Adventures of Muhammad Smith and The Million Man March*

states looking for a Black man in black clothes. Then they found the car she claimed was stolen by a Black man with the bodies of her two sons strapped in with a safety harness to the back seat of a car at the bottom of a lake.

She fessed up, naturally. She was guilty...Through the magic of Court TV you could see the eyes of America almost shedding a tear or two for Susan Smith. In a state with the electric chair Susan got life and was sent to a jail where she had sex with the guards. Seems that other motives existed beyond race.

********

The jury reached a verdict in five hours, four if you don't count lunch. It was beyond belief. How can a 13 month trial end with a four hour deliberation? The restaurant cleared out. People left without ordering as they rushed to find a TV, most likely in their offices, snuck in just like the one in the rear of the restaurant. Traffic on the street seemed to disappear. Everyone was watching the OJ verdict. The cameras appeared with Judge Ito announcing that the jury was present. They had only asked for one piece of evidence during their four hour deliberation. A time line provided by the limousine driver, a seemingly damning turn for OJ Simpson. Now they filed back into the courtroom to an internationally televised OJ Simpson and one of his several lawyers, Carl Douglas. A look of disbelief, complete disbelief...This was it.

There was some nonsense of the foreperson leaving the paperwork in the deliberation room, but beyond that it was just like Perry Mason, or Judd for the Defense.

*Anonymous*

The foreperson gave it to the guard, the guard gave it to the judge who read it, to himself.

Then Carm called.

"Mr. Smith it's for you."

Muhammad hated to leave the TV. He stretched the cord keeping an eye on both the TV and the front.

"Hello. Thank you for calling Fast Food"

"Chuckieee, it's me! Carmillia. Are you watching this, can you believe this?"

"Well until this phone call I was watching and listening. Now I'm onl.."

"Can you believe this?! He is so guilty Chuckie. That man had no right to take that woman's life. I mean the jury reviewed the prosecutions best witnes…AAHHHHHH!"

"AAGGGHHHHHH."

Just then Tamika and the cook who had been watching ran to the front towards Charlie. In frustration Tamika held her fists to her head, but her wide eyes gave indication to the wonder of it all.

"Mr. Smith they ain't gonna read the verdict til tomorrow. The lady said at 1 o'clock, they gonna wait til tomorrow"

"Oh Chuckie I just cannot stand it, the anxiety. That man is going to have a hard time tonight because he is going to jail for life."

"Mr. Smith I feel bad, I want to go home."

"Carm, really this is a bad time. Tamika, work the counter for me and I'll pay you overtime for lunch."

*The Adventures of Muhammad Smith and The Million Man March*

"It ain't right Mr. Smith, they gonna lock him up and throw away the key."
"Chuckie what did that girl say to you?"
"Hey girl it was just a joke."
Their response was harmonious.
"A JOKE!"
And then confusion with clashing words.

"One day they gonna lock your…
"I really"
"…black"
" feel"
"…behind"
"sorry"
"…in"
"for"
"…jail"
"those"
"…Mr."
"people"
"…Smith."
"Chuckie."

"Carm, I gotta go. I'll see you on Sunday." Click. "Tamika hit the counter…Tamika! Hit the counter."

The remainder of the day was filled with customers and employees, walking in a dream state known as the OJ Simpson trial. It was coming to an end by judicial order at 1PM Tuesday, October the third. As Philadelphia, America and even the world counted down every hour to the end of this yearlong march to American justice, Charlie counted the days. Thirteen days from tomorrow "The Million Man March". As he served endless people; Black, White and Puerto Rican with dazzled looks on their faces he thought, he hoped, that thirteen days would be enough time for the races to inflame, Blacks to think, change their mind, buy a ticket (On his bus.) and go to the Million Man March.

# The Beginning of Darkness: BATMAN

"i want drugs.

i want drugs".

She banged the bars with whatever strength she had left. She had sworn off drugs of both the street and prescription kind, she loved all things natural. But after nine hours of labor, today would have to be the exception. MC could only look as the nurses came in injecting her in places he thought they ought not be. But what the heck he was only 17 and this was his first baby. His grandmother had been in the labor room with him but Stephanie screamed that she get out. Now it was only him, Stephanie and whatever was in her belly. Though she was female and only 16 years old, MC was surprised at how hard she squeezed his hand…Scary. He accepted the fact that this was his responsibility for their night of doing "it", but after only one time? Se Le Vie.

********

"Man she always asking you for stuff. Everyday she wants a piece of paper. Just say hello."

Thirteen year old Abraham spoke from experience, Muhammad was still a virgin. As Abe spat out the simplicities MC could only gaze forward with book bag in tow befudled by the complexity of it all.

"Just like that ...'Hello'?"

"Forget it Mac. You don't want none."

"You goin' to school today?"

"I might do homeroom and first period."

"And then what?"

Arms in bemusement

"Hello!"

"So why waste your time with homeroom?"

"I want to see if you gonna talk to Stephanie."

"So that's gonna make your day?"

"Hey Mac, I'm tryin to make your day."

"I know Abe, I know."

"So Mr. Abraham you decided to come to school today or is this a homeroom special?"

"Well I am partial to being special Mrs. Altman."

As Mrs. Altman exhaled in disbelief at the 13 year old, Stephanie tapped Muhammad on the shoulder.

"Can I hold a piece of paper?"

As Stephanie whispered Abraham watched. When MC turned to Stephanie he ran smack dab into his brother's stare.

"Hello" Abraham silently mouthed.

"Having a conversation with our brother Mr. Abraham?"

*The Adventures of Muhammad Smith and The Million Man March*

Mrs. Altman was giving it one last try. Muhammad turned back into his seat. Stephanie's eyes fell to her desk.

"No mam, I'm practicing for the insanity defense. Kinda like a license to just go off."

The class laughed.

"Is that what you're doing with the rest of your life Abraham 'go off' ?"

"I ain't goin' off Mrs. Altman, I'm checking out."

With that he stood, walked and looked his brother in the eye...

"Ain't nothin' new here anyway."

He was gone. Out of the class just like that.

"Mr. Smith if he weren't your twin I would never believe he was your brother."

"Mrs. Altman his name is Muhammad, why don't you call him Mr. Muhammad."

As if his brother hadn't embarrassed him enough, Stephanie was in love."

At the bell homeroom was over and Stephanie rose up and away from MC. He just sat in his seat as the whole class was leaving. He watched as Stephanie walked out the door and then he just did it: Stood up, walked up and...

"Hello."

She turned with a warm smile.

"Hi Muhammad."

"Hi."

...He was speechless. With a blank mind he walked beside her only smiling. The next 43 seconds were excruciating. Thank goodness for the stairwell.

"Well I have to take the stairs to the fourth floor. See you later Muhammad."

Still the warm smile.

"Bye."

Stephanie was in love. Yes she was only thirteen and from certain perspectives she didn't have a clue, but a teenager in love is a logic and power all it's own. Yet it wasn't a physical thing. Stephanie's parents didn't allow television so she developed intellectual aspirations and Muhammad was the only boy in her world who had a clue of what she spoke about. It was 1970 and Vietnam, Watergate and all that sixties stuff was still fresh. They shared a history class and Stephanie was in love.

"Alright class last week we spoke on the American Revolution. What do we remember from that class?"

Muhammad raised his hand.

"Charles."

"The American Revolution was really a sub-war of a global conflict between England and France that really ended with an English victory in India."

"Very good Charles but I so wish you would use British instead of English"

"Why Mr. Conners?"

"Well after all young man it's not the English empire, it's the British Empire."

"Humph."

"I'm going to break you up into groups to review your reports which are due on Thursday."

Standing in the middle of the class he split them in half. Stephanie moved closer to Muhammad.

"OK, this half of the room is one side…The front will be one group and the back will be the other."

And there she sat with Muhammad.

*The Adventures of Muhammad Smith and The Million Man March*

"Muhammad, what's your paper about?"

"Benjamin Franklin."

"Oh, a White man."

"Stephanie who else was there in the American Revolution?"

"Crispus Attucks."

"Crispie who?"

The small group laughed.

"Y'all Black people ain't never heard of Crispus Attucks?"

Larry, with the cocked hat spoke up. "Ain't he some Black dude who got shot?"

"Some Black dude."

She twisted her face.

"He was the first man to die for America and he was a Black Man."

"Muhammad, what Black people do you know in American History?"

Resigned to her logic, MC gave it his best shot.

"John Henry...?"

"My brother, my brother. It's 1970 and you still think the White Man did it all."

Then Donna threw in her two cents.

"Didn't John Henry help to make the railroads?"

"That's how the story goes Donna, but my parents told me all that working hard for America stuff is a lie. My daddy say America ain't never worked hard for me."

Larry still had something to say. "My brother got shot in Vietnam and now he works at the butcher shop on Ridge. He say it's the hardest work he know."

"Stephanie, is Crispus Atkins going to be on the test?"

*Anonymous*

Muhammad, always on task.

"So, what that mean?"

"It means we should get ready for the test."

"This is just a paper, he said we could write about anything from the Revolution, so I'm writing about Crispus Attucks. You can do Benjamin Baneker."

"Stephanie, where do you get these names from?"

Muhammad was perplexed.

"My parents make me read Ebony Magazine."

"But Stephanie, Ebony Magazine ain't gonna be on the test."

"Ben Franklin was born in 1706, so what."

Donna couldn't resist "And he signed the Constitution in 1776"

"Stephanie, why do you always give me a hard time?"

He was serious.

"Because Muhammad is such a pretty name."

No one had ever told him that before.

"Hey Charlie man, what we suppose to be writin' on Thursday?"

Larry was good at breaking the ice.

"The war."

The hallway conversation was more confident now, more relaxed.

"On Saturdays, what do you do?"

"Are you asking me out?"

"No, I just want to know what you do on Saturday."

"I clean up in the morning and then I read. Sometimes my dad takes us to the park. Last week we saw Uptown Saturday Night at the…"

*The Adventures of Muhammad Smith and The Million Man March*

"Cuz, What's Happenin'?" It was Steven Livingston. "Who this fine thing you with cuz?"

"Stevie, this is Stephanie. Stephanie this is Steve, my cousin."

She looked at Steve in awe, maybe fear and at first in silence, with barely a moment to understand the thick darkness of his skin.

"Hey Steph, you got a boyfriend?"

With a toothpick in his mouth the young Stevie looked for an answer, a response.

"Steve, in case you didn't notice we were on our way to class."

"Charlie let the lady speak…Ain't gonna hurt nothin'"

Muhammad had been down this road before.

"Look we gotta go."

With that Muhammad just walked away and fortunately Stephanie followed after a quick, astonished look at Stevie who blew her a kiss.

"That's your cousin?"

"Yeah, kinda."

"And Abraham is YOUR twin"

"Identical"

She gave him the eye.

"You got a weird family. I see you later Muhammad. My class is upstairs. Bye."

She smiled and then giggled up the steps

"Bye"

For Muhammad it served to hide his defeat. The whole thing was a defeat. From Crisspi Atkins to little cousin Steve, a defeat. Her giggling didn't help any. He wasn't Black enough for her and she would never look at him the way she had just looked at Stevie. So what if she asked for paper everyday. What did that mean? That he was a sucker for some indescribable desire he felt whenever a girl was near. 'His family was weird'. What would Abraham say? She was out of his league in a game he didn't want to play.

********

He was born on December 9, 1956.when the Supreme Court ruled on Rosa Parks. Born an identical twin to Abraham Charles Smith they were raised in North Philly near Master and Marshall Streets until they were 12 when they moved to their grandmother's house after Uncle Jay had died. He wouldn't know til years later but his mother was the first on her block to get addicted to heroin. She was a striking figure, both before and after she became a junkie. It's a shame but it's the stuff of life. Pregnant out of wedlock which, even at the age of 16, was stigma in 1956. She retreated to an apartment on Marshall Street and somehow fell into the wrong direction. She said she was in love.

Abraham liked the loud music and the big laughs. For Muhammad the television in his mother's room was his only joy. Batman at 7:30 on a pleasant spring evening in 1968.

In her room his mother also kept a set of encyclopedias. She had nowhere else to keep the gift from her mother. So Muhammad fell into the habit of flipping through the pages whenever TV became a bore or went off at about two in the morning. This is when his mother would come into the room, wanting nothing

*The Adventures of Muhammad Smith and The Million Man March*

more than silence from her son. She would sit there for hours in her bed. Quiet, the two of them.

Abe burst into the room.

"Mommy, Mommmmy! Can I have a quarter?"

"Get out! Get OUT!"

Mary's typical response to everything.

"Batman……..Batman……..Batman…Batman, Batman, Batman."

Mary liked silence at these moments.

Yeah, there was uncle jim, uncle bill and uncle harry. Mary had a whole lot of uncles. But on most days they had enough food to eat and for Muhammad that was good enough. Plus he got free lunch at a special school in Chestnut hill. Well, not really special but White. Seems that his reading really impressed a certain teacher who arranged for him to go to Jenks in Chestnut hill. The education was there for the taking. He got through it well, but not great. He didn't mind the reading but Charlie, Charlie just wanted to cruise on autopilot. Just enough to get by. He was a natural for weed. On their 12$^{th}$ birthday, Abraham challenged Muhammad to a joint.

"Jeffery told me it just makes you dizzy."

"You listenin' to that sissy? Fine I got more for myself."

Right there in the playground on Master Street Abe lit it up. Muhammad walked away to the swings, Abraham followed.

"You just scared."

"Scared of what?"

"Anything that ain't on TV. You scared."

With that Muhammad stopped the swing and grabbed the joint out of Abe's hand and with the same motion took a good deep toke. His bravery got him a terrible coughing spell. But then after his final cough he laughed. He just laughed. Him and his brother laughing til they fell down, still laughing. This was different than autopilot. All of a sudden everything was funny.

Then came the day that mother wasn't there. While this was common, today Grandmom was there along with the cops.

"Abraham, Muhammad your mother is sick. You'll be living with me for a while."

"Why are the cops here?"

"Is that blood?"

"Where's my mommy?"

"Look I have your clothes in the car. Com'on lets go. We'll talk about it later."

"Grandmom, the cops gonna stay at our house? Where's mommy?"

"Is mommy in jail?"

"Is she dead?"

"Is that her blood?"

"No Abraham, it's not her blood!" She cried.

The children continued with their questions but for now she had to cry. It was all so sad.

********

Uncle Jay was no stranger to Mary or her children. Since he first married her mother, Mary and Jay got along just fine. This morning was the exception. The tension at the breakfast table could only be felt by those who knew each other well. Jay sat dressed only in his boxer shorts, not a strange sight for Mac and Abe. Mary put the bowls on the table to a waiting box of cereal and bottle of milk. She wore an oversized men's robe as Jay probed her every move. The kids were eating cereal when she finally sat down.

Jay was the first to speak.

"Mary today I'm takin' you to the clinic."

"Not today Jay. OK. I don't got time for this today. This is foolishness."

"That's what you said yesterday."

"And I say it tomorrow if I feel like it Jay. This is my life."

"Mary you got to get off the stuff."

The kids cocked their eyes when Mary stood straight up.

"Stuff! What 'Stuff'? You mean that junk that you bring up in here for us to have a 'good time' stuff. Ha, ya liked it last night. What's different now, I didn't make you no eggs?"

"Ma, can you make me a bacon sandwich for lunch?"

Abraham always did like Jay.

Mary rolled her eyes and walked away to her room where she slammed the door. Muhammad knew exactly where she was. Once, recently, they had shared a joint in her room. There were no words. She just lit the joint and passed it to him. This may be why he stood up to follow her to her room.

"Mac sit down."

At Jay's command Muhammad sat back down. Jay got up and walked to Mary's bedroom door which was locked.

"Mary open the door."

He knocked strongly at first and then rather hard. He turned back around to the kitchen where Mac and Abe ate breakfast.

"Look you kids get up and go to school."

"But uncle Jay I ain't finished my cereal yet."

"Get up and go to school Abe, now."

With that both boys got up, Muhammad grabbed his books...

"Is mommy going to be alright Uncle Jay?"

"Your mommy is just fine Mac, go on to school."

Before they got to the front door Mac and Abe could hear Jay pounding on the door.

"Open this door Mary."

They went off. They would never know it but shortly after they left Jay Livingston had begun the last moments of his life. Within seconds he was kicking on the door.

"Open the door Mary."

His whole body went into the door, not once but twice, and then it was open. She was on the bed with a needle almost in her arm. But looking at Jay through the door, she knew it was time to move. With a quick acceleration, she rose from the bed, with needle in her hand and a band across her arm.

"Leave me alone Jay."

She tried to dart to the other side but he blocked her off.

"You want some of this Mary. You want to feel good Mary."

*The Adventures of Muhammad Smith and The Million Man March*

He threw her back to the bed. Then he punched her.

"Aghhww! Aghhww aghhww!"

He only hit her once but she screamed several times as she squiggled away and again tried for the other side. He rushed straight to the door, blocking all escape.

"Aghhww! Aghhww! Stay away from me, stay away!"

He approached her directly. Feeling cornered she held her ground and while keeping a strong eye on him she placed the needle to her arm.

"Stay away from me Jay."

"That's all you want ain't it Mary. You don't want kids, you don't want this apartment. You don't even want me. You going to the clinic today."

With that he rushed her. She ran to the dresser and opened the draw.

"What you gonna do with that? Put that thing away girl."

"Stay away from me Jay."

With a nickel plated gun in one hand she pushed the last of the drug into her arm. In her brief relief he pounced on her. The gun went off several times. She was crazy. One shot got him, in the eye. Like a sack of rocks he dropped.

********

Muhammad and his brother Abraham got to see their mother one last time at Byberry State hospital with a straight jacket on and so sedated she didn't recognize the boys or her mother when they entered the visitor's room. Abraham was startled when she sprang up and ran for the door. But the attendants quickly put her in her place. Muhammad was calm and once back in her seat he spoke.

"Hello mommy."

Without looking she spoke.

"Muhammad is that you baby?"

"Yeah mom, it's me."

"Mommy loves you baby."

Mary couldn't look him in the eye. Maybe she was ashamed because her hair was a wreck or maybe it was the memory of what they once had.

"Mommy loves you baby."

"Mommy when are we going back to Marshall Street?"

"Mommy loves you baby."

While this was getting old, everyone noticed that she started to rock. Muhammad was starting to cry. His sadness though was quiet.

"Mommy loves you Muhammad."

Then she started to cry in a dramatic way, she was sobbing

"Mommy is so sorry baby."

"Grandmom can we go now."

Muhammad ignored his brother but when Mary leaned towards them the attendants grabbed her, dragging her from the room ranting.

"Mommy loves you. Mommy loves you. Mommy loves you."

She fought the attendants, screaming with every step as her family could only look on to a closing door.

Mary was gone from his life.

# A Sign of Hope: JULIA

The next real woman in his life would be Stephanie Morgan of Duvall Street. She had first eyed him at the pharmacy on Green and Duvall. For her it was the Sunday paper, him a prescription for his Grandmother. It was only an eye to the oblivious Muhammad Charles Smith. To her at the early age of maybe eleven, as she remembered it, she saw a certain 'certainness' to his calm demeanor. She was wearing a beautiful, multi-colored, patterned African dress. He wore the plain blue suit of a Negro child fresh from Sunday School. When they would meet again in the homeroom of their 9th grade class, Stephanie would remember this day.

After they met in the 9th grade they managed to sign up for the same school trips to museums, plays and the Liberty Bell. She secretly admired his knowledge of all things European. In reality, Muhammad didn't know the names of all the Greek gods, but just the fact that he knew that's where this whole "White" thing started impressed her. The sculptured forms cast in the purist of ivory. The rising columns of solid marble and the simple lie of Helen of Troy. Muhammad claimed that history was a never ending story right up to today's headlines. And while Stephanie didn't know much about Rome she knew that Hannibal defeated them with Elephants, from Africa. She didn't know what happened before or since Rome but she knew about Africa. She knew of the Zulu and the claimed Egyptians. For every Lincoln that Muhammad could name, Stephanie would counter with a Frederick Douglas and if she could she would throw in Nat Turner as well. Muhammad had barely heard of the Cato Conspiracy or Harriet Tubman. And when he did learn of such people he brushed them off as so much insignificance.

Even at the age of thirteen Muhammad saw all things Negro as hopeless attempts to be White. His mother subscribed to Life magazine, something about giving her kids 'culture'. At his grandmother's house it was Ebony magazine. Right off the bat the cover was the same: A picture with a red square white letter logo. But almost from page one they were as different as day and…dawn. 'Life' pictured the never ending advancement, beauty and purity of what Charlie came to know as Western civilization. Even their empathy for the American Negro was pictured with cute little Black girls, dressed in black at a family church. Then there was 'Ebony', page three. Charlie came to see it as the "First Black Man to be White" page. It was filled on a monthly basis, for years, with Negroes who were the first in their ever-narrowing fields. In 1965 it would be the first Negro to be on the Cabinet. By 1970 it was the first Black to head the Welfare Department in Detroit, Michigan. Muhammad could see that progress was being made.

*The Adventures of Muhammad Smith and The Million Man March*

But deep in his gut there was a secret that he would not share even with his brother on their best of days. Deep in his very core belief of...everything, Muhammad felt that Blacks, Colored, Negroes, Afro-Americans or whatever you wanted to call them, were inherently dumb. It was a thought so clear to him that he came to hate the very act of thinking. From Sammy 'half Puerto Rican' Davis being the "Black" Frank Sinatra to the processed hair that Uncle Jay and all the Temptations wore on their head: Feeble attempts at being equal to White. Once, in class the subject was Albert Einstien. Out of the blue Stephanie said George Washington Carver. A button was pushed.

"What, how can you compare George Washington Carver to Einstien! I mean...what like an Apple and a orange? How can you make that comparison? Einstein helped make the A-Bomb and what, Carver invented the peanut?"

The teacher nodded in complete agreement with Charlie.

"It wasn't the peanut, it was peanut oil."

"So he invented oil?"

Then she went racial.

"You don't know nothin' about being Black do you Muhammad? You don't even like me calling you Muhammad do you?"

"I'm not sayin all that. I'm saying that as far as advancing civilization..."

"Civilization, you mean like the slaves, right?"

"Now it's a slave thing. We went from Einstein to the slaves...I give up, you win."

Their juvenile minds could articulate no further than that. But the conversation was far from over and besides they liked each other. After class, during lunch Stephanie tried to defend herself.

"Muhammad, you remember that documentary on TV about three years ago and they got those kids to say they didn't want to be Black?"

Everybody remembered that documentary. In fact the only reason they knew the definition of the word documentary was because of that documentary. It was a powerful profile on how inter-city children perceived their racial identity. Regardless of your beliefs on various racial theories it was obvious that these Black children did not want to be Black. To the point of tears they made these proud, educated Black children admit the truth: They wanted to be White. Everybody remembered that documentary.

"Yeah, I remember."

"Muhammad we have to be proud of being Black because we are Black."

"Like the James Brown song, say it over and over and over again. Then it will come true. Right Stephanie?"

"Muhammad that's not what I'm saying."

"OK, What are you saying?"

"I'm saying that Black people did things too."

"OK, What?"

"Like, like...George Washington Carver."

"And what did he do?"

"He showed that there was more to something than meets the eye."

"The eye of what? The eye of a peanut? That doesn't compare to inventing the light bulb. And no matter what you say, that's a fact."

"So I guess one day they gonna invent a peanut hunh?"

"Yeah, one day they just might. After all the study of genetics began with the pea."

"Muhammad, when are you ever going to learn?"

"When you explain it to me."

********

Even though the horror of recent history from Jim Crow to Bull Conner was fresh in everyone's minds it was 1970 and everybody could vote, sit in the front of the bus and Dianne Carrol was Julia on TV: Supposedly the first Black with their own TV show. Muhammad didn't see the problem. He didn't see what the fuss was about. The concept of the last hired and first fired didn't occur to him. The massive fact that Edison High School in the heart of Black North Philly had more students killed in Vietnam than any other high school in America meant nothing to Muhammad. The constant parade of Black criminals on the local televised news went over his head like an international offshore tax shelter. The numerous construction projects manned to the last man by a White man. And as his little mind could not see the massive paychecks earned by these construction workers doing stereotypical "Black" work, Muhammad's little eyes clearly saw that Black men only wore suits on Sunday. Even then Muhammad saw nothing wrong. And if anything was wrong, the White man would fix it. That's how he saw it in 1970.

*Anonymous*

Martin Luther King was cute but it was a White man who signed the law. In fact, for Muhammad, MLK was much ado about nothing. When he was killed in '68 non-violence was already dead. Riots seemed to be the norm and a yearly occurrence. King at that point was far from the page one headlines of the late fifties, before Muhammad could even remember. If Martin Luther King appeared in the papers at all before April '68 it was on page 19…A trash man's strike. (By May they had their contract. It was on page one.)

Yes there were questions in Charlie's mind: Why were all the cops White? If there were ever a Black genius as there had been White geniuses, what place would there be in history or downtown Philly for that Black genius? And even though all trash men were Black, Muhammad knew that the men in his life from Uncle Jay to his cousin James were far more than trash men.

Still there was one event in the course of his short life that he couldn't deny. Street vendors had become an issue in the Philadelphia of 1970. The city in the person of Mayor Frank Rizzo had declared them illegal. Yet on the radio, WDAS the black radio station, he heard that White men like Gimbels and Wanamaker had made their first fortune from street vending and went on to build their respectable department stores. And while it would be another ten years before Negroes would discover how much profit could be made from selling hot dogs on the street, the very fact that Negroes dared to sell anything on the street was deemed illegal. People like John and Milton Street made their careers from this one issue. Because before they became accomplished politicians, they were street vendors.

It was Muhammad and Abraham walking down Market Street just past 13$^{th}$ when they saw with their adolescent eyes the cops swoop down in front of Wanamaker's Department Store, throw a vendor's goods to the ground and then throw a vibrant, kicking and screaming Black woman into the paddy wagon. The way she was kicking they were sure to charge her with more than "vending without a license". It didn't make the 11 o'clock news or the morning paper. Right there Muhammad knew that if it were a Black man he would of praised the cops and it would most definitely of been in the morning paper "Crazed Negro Attacks Police". But the very fact that it was a Black woman maybe ten years older than him made him see things in a different light. Perhaps like the four little Birmingham girls who had died about ten years earlier had made America think twice. In spite of the fact that all of his studies had told him different, Muhammad knew that there was some validity to being Black: Something more to Black than Wilt Chamberlin scoring 100 points. Being that it was Philly they didn't talk about Bill Russel that much.

For Abraham it was simple.

"Guess she picked the wrong day to be Black. Come on man lets go."

Muhammad wanted to stay to see the door on the paddy wagon close. There was more to this than being Black on the wrong day…His thinking mind just wouldn't stop.

Thinking: It grew to be a pain.

They lived with their Grandmother now and of the many things that that meant it included going to church every Sunday. For Abraham it was outright boredom. For Muhammad it was an intellectual exercise that had run it's course: Devil, Saint, Heaven and Hell. Over and over again that's all he heard. For both of them Grandmom's church didn't mean salvation it meant keeping Grandmom happy…Nothing else. Now at the age of 15, Grandmom's days of making them go to church were coming to an end. Perhaps this would be their last Sunday. The 2nd Street AME Church was 70% filled on any given Sunday mostly with Grandmothers and their grandchildren. Then there was Easter when the church would overflow because the parents suddenly got religion.

Today wasn't Easter though and the sermon was given by the grandson of the Pastor, Elijah Baker the Third. At the AME church they were big on that: 'So and so' the Third and 'such and such' the Fourth. Charlie figured it made them feel important.

Whatever…Charlie watched as Reverend Baker took to the pulpit and began what Charlie hoped would be a quick sermon.

"Can I get an Amen?"

Placing his bible on the podium the routine began.

"amen."

"I Said Can I Get a AMEN!

"AMEN"

"Well alright, thank you Jesus."

There always was the echo from various members of the congregation.

"Thank you Jesus, thank you lord"

*The Adventures of Muhammad Smith and The Million Man March*

"I don't want to take up too much of your time today, I know the Eagles are playing New York today."

For Muhammad this was a sure sign that the sermon would be long. Abraham just went to sleep. Muhammad held a slight attraction for the oratory styles of the different preachers who visited their church. And this, being the pastor's grandson, was the youngest he had ever seen.

"Ain't that right Granddaddy, the Eagles is playin' them Giants today?"

Pastor Baker waved his hand in agreement as Elijah turned back to the congregation.

"Today I want to talk about the greatest giant known to man. And that would be...Can I get an Amen."

A wipe of the brow.

"I said can I get an AMEN?"

The typical response...

"AMEN."

"The greatest giant known to mankind."

The 'everything is relative' routine.

"Is the giant foundation at the very core of our religious belief."

From football to God with only two amens. This kid was better than his Grandfather...Muhammad was impressed. Abraham slept.

"Now this mornings I wants you to open your bible to the first sheet of paper."

The reverend performed this task slowly but with great confidence, in fact with a swagger.

"Today we need not the verse for we start at the very foundation of all that we believe. Can I get an Amen."

A lone voice responds.

"Amen..."

"We start before Cain slew Able, before the great wars of Jerico and before Jesus was white..."

"AMEN, AMEN!"

The amens were spontaneous on that one, in fact old sister Rivers sprang to her feet..

"We beginnnnn back before Samson knew the charms of Deliah and before Lazurus could feel the sting of death. We begin with the very first sheet of paper written so many years ago by wise, old men."

With his flowing robe he turns to his Grandfather sitting behind him.

"Grandfather, can I get a Amen?"

The old man smiled as the humor of amen flowed from the congregation.

"Go on son."

Elijah turns back to the crowd.

"My friends I wants you to take that sheet of paper and turn to page...two...The first page speaks to the creation, and we all revel in that, so well...No today my friends I wish to speak upon the original, the first sin and transgression of man against God....Thee initial... instigator as they would say."

"...Amen..."

Abraham had a way of sleeping that his grandmother behind them could not see. Nor could she see the intent interest in Charlie's face.

"I wants you to focus your god given eyes and look to verse...TWO SEVENTEEN"

"Amen"

Came a lone female voice

"I see that Sister Nora May is ahead of the game, As always....BUT OF THE TREE OF **KNOWLEDGE**

*The Adventures of Muhammad Smith and The Million Man March*

OF GOOD AND EVIL You shall not eat. For in the day that you eat from it you shall Surely Die."

"Amen…"

"No my brothers and my sisters, I need more than a amen. I want to hear you read the words…..BUT…"

As always the group reading was disjointed yet they sputtered it out anyway.

"But from the tree of knowledge of good and evil you shall not eat for in the day that you eat from it you shall surely die."

"Was it the tree of evil?"

He was on a roll now.

"Was it the tree of good times to come?

"No." The congregation was on the same page now.

"The tree of rape, plunder and death?

"No"

"Was it a apple tree, turnip green tree or a sweet potato pie tree that that devil slithered down, the lonnnng and the winding road tempting the lovely dammmmsel in her garden. A garden of Eden, a garden of God… A garden with a snake."

"Amen…"

"He smiled, that devil. He smiled that devil…And he said to that lovely damsel in her heavenly bliss, that he so despised. I said the devil despised that heavenly bliss. And he SAID: Woman hear me

"I know a tree.

"A tree like no other

"There in the middle of the garden.

"In the middle of the garden

"I know a tree

"A tree that will make you God

81

*Anonymous*

"Be like God,
"Talk like God
"A tree that will make you God.
"And the Damsel smiled
"To be like God, to Talk like God, Walk like God. A tree that will make me God.
"So she took a nibble,
"Just one small nibble,
"But it was the nibble of Death from the tree of Knowledge
"And the devil smiled
"And the woman turned to Adam and he ate of the tree, thinkin' he was god
"But only found that he was naked.
"And God came
"And God saw
"And God SAID
"Of all that is good and evil
"How is it that you know that you are naked?
"And Adam pointed to Eve
"And Eve pointed to the Devil
"But the Devil pointed to the tree.
"The tree of knowledge
"Of Gooood and E-vile.
"The Knowledge of all we know
"And Dream of
"And hope for
"The tree of Knowledge
"The knowledge of good and evil."

He took a breather his sweaty face looking at the congregation with a smile.

"Lord they was some finger pointin' people back then"

*The Adventures of Muhammad Smith and The Million Man March*

"…Amen!…"

"Make me glad I wasn't back there with that there tree of Knowledge. I might have to start pointin' my finger at y'all."

"…Well…"

"My brothers and sisters, the answers we seek are not where we think them to be. We have been deceived by a world of small print and buy one get one free. We have been deceived by a belief that the A-Bomb will solve all our problems as we turn away from our god. How modern is modern, my brothers and my sisters?"

He smiled a smile.

"Not to take up to much of your time my brothers and my sisters but please turn to the last verse of chapter two, Genesis two twenty four: So He drove the man out and at the east of Eden He stationed the flaming sword which turned in every direction, to guard the way to the tree of life."

'The tree of knowledge'.
Muhammad's life was forever changed.

\*\*\*\*\*\*\*\*

"Muhammad call the nurse"
Stephanie was still weak.
"Hunh?"
"CALL THE NURSE i pooped"
He pushed the button and then rushed to the hall and then to the nurses station.
"Miss my wife…she pooped in the bed."
"Oh she'll be fine."
She kept typing.

"But…."

"There's some napkins in the room if you want them, right next to the mirror."

Back to her typing.

Muhammad turned all wide-eyed and made his way steadily back to the room and to the side of the mirror. Thick heavy duty napkins…He dug in.

It was seven o'clock in the morning and throughout the night he had managed sleep between the contractions. Once she started the epid-doral she also began to sleep between contractions. Even though they both had promised throughout the pregnancy not to use drugs he was glad see her relaxed instead of the high-octane performance she put on last night: Screaming, squeezing his hand, the dramatic promises, kicking his grandmother out. When she banged on the bed and demanded drugs, Muhammad knew it was her call. She was on the front line and he wasn't about to even mention anything about a drug free existence.

"Ahhhhh"

It was another contraction

"Muhammad."

She was actually crying. He dutifully rose to her side.

"Just stand here baby, just stand here."

Now the nurse comes in.

"Good morning. You feel another one coming on?

"YEs."

More of a groan than a word.

"How did you know?"

He was full of questions.

*The Adventures of Muhammad Smith and The Million Man March*

"We monitor the heartbeat from down the hall. She'll be due any minute now. We're going to move her into the prep room."

With that she manipulated the bedding as a crew of two other nurses came into the 'Labor' room to move them to the prep room. The prep room was more like a doctors exam room at the neighborhood clinic. A lot less comfortable than the carpeted and furnished Labor room.

They dressed her in a hospital gown, cleaned her up and put her into a different bed. The contractions were coming quickly so they had to hurry. They pointed to a stool and told Muhammad to sit there and then they left.

"Muhammad."

She appeared to be calm.

"Yeah?"

"Come here, I'm not going to bite you. Look at me."

Muhammad did as he was told.

"I love you"

"I love you too."

"We gonna raise this baby to be somethin' special."

"Yeah, something special. Ok."

"I'm serious. I'm gonna be there for him and you too. Right?"

And so it began.

********

Before he even left the church he was transfixed by the concept that knowledge itself was not the perfection he thought it was. The perfection upon which everything rests: From the perfection of money to the perfection of science. Before he even left the church he realized how all around him this whole knowledge thing led more to confusion than anything else; The endless translations of the Bible and the King James VERSION, the un-certain promise of nuclear energy, the meaning of soul.

For the following week he was focused as he rarely was. This knowledge thing...This Black thing. Something wasn't right. Black People don't say "good hair" because they might say silky by accident. Then they shout Nigger as if it were the grit and grime of day to day life. White People want hair with body but they dare not say Nigger because no matter how nice they say it, it comes off as a sub-human speices. But there's one thing that both dare not say, for it strikes at the very core of racist policies. And as Grandmom would say "You touchin' my last nerve". During this whole dis-jointed national, local, thanksgiving dinner conversation on race the one subject that is never mentioned is 'intelligence'. No one dared say in public, or private, that the White Man was smarter than the Black Man. And even though he did not question his own intelligence Muhammad wondered why the best that Blacks could offer to Da Vinci, Einstein or the local Science teacher was George Washington Carver: A pretty name and a peanut. Why was it that Whites were always the first in line for this, this, this perfection?

PERFECTION! It was on the walk to school when it hit him out of the blue. Abraham was talking to Darlene and Charlie was up ahead a bit, just to the right. He spun around to Abraham and proclaimed:

*The Adventures of Muhammad Smith and The Million Man March*

"Knowledge, the curse of Mankind!"

This only got him blank stares from Abraham and Darlene.

"Your brother got issues Abraham."

"And you got melons."

He reached for her chest, she continued the flirtation with a soft slap to Abe's hand. Charlie turned back forward with a smile. But as soon as he sat in Mrs. Altman's homeroom class he raised his hand.

"Yes Charles."

"Mrs. Altman is there such a thing as perfection."

"No there's no such thing."

"Then why did they make the atom bomb?"

"To end the war."

"The Vietnam war?"

"Charles what are you talking about?"

"I'm just figuring out that it don't matter if the Black Man is dumb because smart, ain't smart."

"Nigger."

"Boy."

"Fool."

Everyone in class jumped on his case from the delinquent to Stephanie. Even his brother looked on with a distance.

"Mac man cool out with that Niggers is dumb stuff."

"Abe, you care? You who said that Blacks can't figure out how to park on the Parkway and did 55 in the driveway."

"I did not."

"Yeah, you right. You actually said NIGGERS couldn't park on the Parkway."

"Why you so new Mac? What's up?"

What was up was that Abraham was Charlie's easiest way out. The reaction when he said it was ok to be dumb, ok for Blacks to be dumb, was a flame he did not imagine.

"How do you say it Abe…Nigger Please"

"OK Charles that's enough of the "N" word. In fact I'm going to take roll now. Does anyone have a problem with that?"

Within a year, massive thoughts flooded into Muhammad's head ranging from the Northern and Southern Hemispheres, The Industrial Revolution to the latest Selectric Typewriter from IBM. All that he had learned and realized from flipping through the pages of an old Encyclopedia, the Yellow Pages and the bicycle section of the Sears catalog lead him to a unique understanding of the first transgression of man against god: Knowledge. It would take him twenty years to finally and completely articulate it but in spite of his ability to read he now knew that knowledge wasn't all that it was cracked up to be.

# As The World Turns: GENERAL HOSPITAL

The contractions were less than 3 minutes apart. The nurses came rushing in.

"OhhKay. It's time."

"Time for what?" He spoke up.

"The baby is comin' Muhammad! The baby its comin', I can feel it Muhammad."

"Are you coming into the birth room?..." The nurse glanced at his papers "...Mr. Smith?"

The nurse's question demanded a quick answer.

"...Yeah, sure I'm going in."

"Thank you Muhammad, Thank yoouuu, ummmph."

What she was thanking him for, he didn't know but just like that she went into another contraction. They quickly grabbed her bed, took off the brakes and were off to a room a few doors away.

The doctor was a woman who quickly took control.

"Stephanie, is that your name, Stephanie?"

"...Yes, yes. help me with my baby. please help me with my baby."

*Anonymous*

"OK Stephanie I'm Doctor Jackson and here's what I need you to do. On your next contraction you have push. Just like you're doing a number two in the bathroom. Push."

"Oh, oh it's coming it ummmmmmmmph."

Her eyes furrowed, her teeth clenched. Her hands were balled up into tight little wads of intense effort.

A 17 year old Muhammad stood off to the side.

And just like that another contraction.

"Come on Stephanie, you have to push harder."

"uggggggggggumph"

After a quick exhale she inhaled into tears.

"It won't come out. my baby won't come out. Ohhh Doctor it hurts, it hurts.

Uggggggemph"

She was giving her all and then a surge of blood. It literally spurted into the doctor's face.

"I got a flow here! I'm going to need some shears here"

The doctor spoke with authority, which was all that Muhammad had to calm him. The whole pace of the room had gone from routine to excited in the space of seconds, about two seconds after Stephanie let out a scream. The doctor stepped back as a nurse gave Stephanie several injections with one needle. Another nurse gave the doctor what appeared to be stainless steel shears. The injections were finished and the doctor actually dove between Stephanie's legs with a pair of cutting shears. Almost to Muhammad's horror he could actually see the doctor's arm cutting into Stephanie and several sprinkles of blood sprinkling, everywhere.

"Shears!"

*The Adventures of Muhammad Smith and The Million Man March*

Like that a nurse took them away and the doctor quickly returned her hand back between Stephanie's legs.

"Here it comes. Here comes mommy's little baby…. Head nurse!"

A nurse sprang forward and grabbed the baby. The baby. Stephanie almost was oblivious, exhausted. Breathing sighs more so than air.

"Are you the father?"

The same nurse who asked if he was coming to the birth room now turned with another direct question.

"Yeah… I guess so. First time I been called a father."

"Well you have a son."

"Can I see?"

"Of course you can."

Muhammad stepped up to the table to see a dark skinned human baby.

"It's so dark."

"Oh that, they're never the same color when they grow up. Look at the ears"

The nurse assured him.

"Nobody in my family is that dark."

"Oh. You'll have to excuse us now Mr. Smith."

They bundled the child up and took him off to a clinic and then quickly to the nursery. There Stephanie's parents and his grandmother could google over the baby…But he would later find out that his grandmother was of the same mind as he.

"That baby is Black."

"This is a lovely black man child."

"Nobody in my family is that Black."

*Anonymous*

"Excuse me Miss Smith is there a problem with this child being 'Black'".

Stephanie's father who at that very moment was wearing a Dashiki couldn't take any more.

"Oh no it's a lovely child...Lovely baby."

Like that the families were forever split.

********

When MC told Christians, like his grandmother, that knowledge was the first sin, they all responded in the same way, every single last one of them maintained that it wasn't knowledge that so upset god but disobedience. When he told his teachers they merely said that this wasn't a catholic school and such God and Jesus talk wasn't necessary. In spite of his off the wall theory, Muhammad was suddenly much more receptive to Stephanie's tilted view of history. They were sixteen and would never realize til years later that they were...sixteen. In school, on a trip or strolling in Fairmount Park they were sixteen.

"I'm telling you Muhammad if it wasn't for the Black Man there would be no America"

"How you figure that Stephanie? What logic of history told you that?"

"My daddy says..."

"Oh it's daddy. Some of that African logic hunh?"

"My daddy says that if the White Man didn't have niggers to kick around they would of kicked themselves into World War Four."

"Your Daddy is a racist."

"My daddy says that black people can't be racists"

"Oh yeah, why's that?"

*The Adventures of Muhammad Smith and The Million Man March*

"Because Black people can't join the Klu Klux Klan, that's why."

"They can join the Black Panthers."

"But that's different."

"How?"

"It took the cops 100 years to get the Klu Klux Klan. They arrested the Black Panthers in five months."

"Well whippy do. That's one for you and one…."

Suddenly he dove in for a kiss. She dodged as if swatting a fly.

"Muhammad what are you doing?"

"I'm trying to kiss you."

"You gonna kiss me by jumping on me?"

"I just wanted to surprise you."

"You can't jump on people Muhammad. That's not love."

"So what am I suppose to do Stephanie, ask you?"

"And what's wrong with that?"

"Never mind……………………I heard you kissed my cousin Steve."

"That's not true. Who told you that."

"Steve."

"Why that liar. Wait til I see him again, I'll…"

"So like, you see him on a regular basis?"

"No he's just in my Spanish class."

"Oh."

"I thought you didn't like girls Muhammad. We been going on trips for two years and you never tried to kiss me before."

"I guess I just didn't want to jump on you before. That's all"

"Awww I see you all mad and everything."

"How come you never tried to kiss me Stephanie?"

"Because you never asked. Shoot I don't know what you want to do boy."

"Mad. What me mad, why because you kissed Stevie? Naw I'm not mad."

"…………..Well, do you want to kiss me Muhammad?"

"Naw, that's ok. Just forget it."

She stepped in front of him, blocking his way.

"Kiss me Muhammad."

She closed her eyes…He hesitated. Her eyes popped open.

"KISS me."

She waited with puckered lips and then felt a peck against her cheek. When Stephanie opened her eyes Muhammad was five feet down the lane.

"Have you ever kissed a girl Muhammad?"

"Stephanie, you're the only Black girl I ever knew."

Her smile was innocent but he was unsure and somehow hurt. When she giggled he felt embarrassed.

"Look I, I got to go, I got a report to do. I'll see you in school on Monday."

She never caught up to him as he ran off. By time she had called his name a second time he had already crossed Lincoln Drive. He had wanted more…So did she. There was no call on Sunday afternoon as was usually the case with them and by time Monday homeroom came they politely avoided each other. There would have been history class later that afternoon if not for what Charlie saw during lunch. He saw Stevie in a hallway clear from across the cafeteria. His dark

*The Adventures of Muhammad Smith and The Million Man March*

laughing face contrasted nicely with the light-skinned smile of Stephanie. For the first time in his life he cut class, not the whole day, just History class. That night Stephanie called him at home.

"Charlie, the phone is for you."

"I'll get it up here Grandmom."

He walked to her bedroom and picked up the line.

"Hello."

"Muhammad?"

"What do you want Stephanie?"

She was surprised by the bland nature of his voice.

"You weren't in History class today…I need help with the homework. Can you help me Muhammad? Can you help me tonight?"

"………..OK I'll meet you at the library in thirty minutes."

"No I can't go to the library tonight. You have to come over here."

"………..What's the assignment?"

"We talked about the Industrial Revolution."

"Mass Production, 1876."

"Are you going to help me Muhammad?"

"Thirty minutes."

He hung up the phone almost in disgust.

DING DONG. Stephanie opened the door as Miss Harris watched from next door.

"Hello Stephanie."

"Hello Muhammad."

She turned leaving the door open. He knew the way.

"How come your dad ain't playin' that jazz stuff?"

*Anonymous*

"Mommy and Daddy aren't here, they at a meeting for the community center. We can sit in the living room if you want."

He sat. She beside him, academically.

"Chapter nine right?"

"Yes Muhammad, chapter nine."

They turned their books

"OK, you got the establishment of railroads in America…"

"Yes Muhammad."

"…New products like the telephone, telegraph."

"Yes Muhammad."

"In America it's the end of the civil war. In Europe the kings are gone and people are doing what they want to do."

"Yes Muhammad."

It was undeniable, if he turned in her direction her lips would be right there.

"Everything was in place for mass production and mass consumption."

"Yes Muhammad."

She was even closer now.

"Industrialization took hold, it was like the mechanization of the planet Earth."

"Yes Mu…."

He did it. He turned and he kissed her and he wasn't going to let go. Her hands gently held his head to her lips. He never did feel her tightening grip across his back. He only wanted to kiss her, his hands to her waist, his body so near. A natural gravity pulled them down, irresistible to both. Soon he was upon her, kissing her neck. When she bit his ear a quiver went through his body forcing his hips to suddenly thrust forward. He would of felt out of place if not for the fact that she thrust her hips back to him and still they kissed. He had heard Abe and some of the guys talk of this sex thing. This was real. THIS WAS REAL. She still wore the dress she had on in school, a modest dress that went below her knees. She had it above her waist in two seconds and forced his hands to her buttocks. She knew what she wanted. As Muhammad squeezed and pushed the soft gentle flesh she fumbled at his belt, but they wouldn't stop kissing...They were only sixteen. Cursing the fool who invented belts Muhammad ripped it off with pants to his thighs and his underwear stretched down, feeling only the wet cotton of her panties. Shortly she removed even that. They kissed with abandon but their hips had found their own rhythm. THIS WAS REAL, and it felt good.

"Thank you Stephanie, Thank You Stephanie, Thank you."

"Kiss me Muhammad."

There they were naked in that certain way. Home without parents at that silly age of sixteen.

Maybe an hour later she opened the door with her hair slightly amiss. His pants wouldn't fasten properly as the snap had been ripped off. The perky smiles on their faces though spoke little of ruffled hair and pants ajar.

"Goodnight Stephanie."

"Goodnight Muhammad."

He stole a kiss, she offered her tongue. He smiled and walked home, almost skipped. He had finally got some...What could be better?

\*\*\*\*\*\*\*\*

Two weeks later she told him she was pregnant in the school hallway.

"Pregnant!? Really?"

She only shook her head.

"How you know so soon. I mean your stomach's not getting' big or nothin' "

"I missed my period."

"You seen the doctor, did the doctor say so?"

"I missed my period. Will you come with me to the doctor?"

"What!"

"Come with me to the doctor."

"You're pregnant Stephanie?"

His eyes couldn't believe his frustration.

"Yes. I'm pregnant. Now what are you going to do about it Black Man?"

"What am 'I' going to do about it. How the heck I know, you the one who pregnant. Why don't your mom go with you, what the hell can I do?"

"My parents don't know about it. Besides I'm sixteen, I can do this by myself."

"So go to the doctor by yourself...Stephanie, you really pregnant?"

"Stop asking me that. We both made this baby and we bringin' it in right with a mommy and a 'Daddy'."

He walked away….

"Look I'll call you tonight, I got to get away from this."

In the crowded hallway Stephanie stood alone.

\*\*\*\*\*\*\*\*

*The Adventures of Muhammad Smith and The Million Man March*

Eight months later she was sedated from the drugs she swore she'd never take. Stephanie lied in bed surrounded by her family. Muhammad was at her bedside, her parents behind him. His Grandmother stayed at the foot of the bed with cousin James.

"Stephanie it's a boy. Do you hear me it's a boy."

She nodded and smiled.

"You did a fine job honey."

Her Father chimed in his support.

"Now you kids got to do the right thing and get married. Gots to bring this child up right."

"Yes Mr. Morgan."

"You can call me Saleed son."

"Muhammad that's Mr. Morgan's new African name."

His wife loved him so.

"Ah Charlie can I see you for a moment dear."

The Morgans cast an eye to Sally Smith but with a resolute frown on her mouth it was obvious to the Morgans and Charlie that she meant now.

"Just for a minute darling."

"Yes Grandmom?"

In the hallway she spoke.

"Boy I want you to get a blood test."

"For what grandmom?"

"A paternity test boy. That ain't you're baby."

"What are you talking about Grandmom."

"That baby is too dark to be your baby. That girl's parents is lighter than she is. That ain't your baby Charlie!"

"Grandmom I got to get back in there."

"Young man you're going up to that desk and ask that nurse for a blood test."

Resolute.

It was simple, a needle prick, a vial of blood and 24 hours later the results. Two days earlier, he had planned on applying himself better in school. To achieve the "A's" he knew were well within his grasp. To set a goal for himself, his family and the mother of his child, his son, the soon to be named Muhammad Charles Smith.... Jr. Just two days earlier, beyond the intensity of birth, he had begun the concept of love. What he felt for the kicks he felt through her womb was responsibility. She fluttered on thoughts of a crib and a bedroom set. All Charlie could see was the need for a job. Her parents were being very nice about the whole affair. But his grandmother cursed the day she met Stephanie. Two days earlier there were so many decisions. Now, with his grandmother behind him and Stephanie in front of him, it all fell to one 24 hour result.

"Here you are Mr. Smith."

It was the same nurse who had asked him, if he wanted to go into the Birth room. All along it was the same nurse. Still Muhammad couldn't piece it together and had no clue what the paper just shoved into his hand was.

"The results Mr. Smith…, from the paternity test."

His grandmother and James watched as the paper changed hands.

**SUBJECT:** Baby, Male, Stephanie Morgan.

**PROCEDURE:** Verification, Paternity

**RESULT:** Negative

**3ʳᵈ PARTY:** Smith, Muhammad C.

"Sir what does 'Negative' mean?"

"It means that if you had been thinking with the head on your shoulders instead of the head between your legs you wouldn't be in this mess."

James could be cruel.

"It means that you ain't the daddy."

His Grandmother was clear.

Speechless, Muhammad was speechless. The nurse just walked past him and said...

"Mmmmm, happens every time."

Regardless he was still speechless, walking into Stephanie's room it was all so...blank.

"Good Morning Muhammad...Sr."

Stephanie's father was in a particularly good mood.

"Humph!"

Grandmom Sally was in rare form and the look on Charlie's face hid the small piece of paper in his hand.

"Muhammad..."

Mrs. Morgan was a gentle soul.

"...what's the matter?"

He looked to her with a certain sadness and held to her the small piece of paper. After brief seconds she glanced over it and rushed from the room in tears, dropping the paper. Stephanie was shocked.

"Mom! Mother!...Muhammad what's wrong?"

Mr. Morgan picks up the piece of paper and runs to his wife...

"Dorothy, DOROTHY!"

"Muhammad what's wrong, why is my mother crying. What's wrong Muhammad?"

He could only look at her, with…the child.

"Muhammad talk to me. What's going on here?"

She demanded an answer.

"He is not the father of that child and the paternity test proves it."

Sally Brown Smith spoke. Stephanie inhaled with never-ending shock but at the first breath she began to cry. She turned away but still Muhammad looked. This would come to be a lifetime memory for him. For the rest of his life he would always remember the sight of her crying, alone, with that little dark baby.

# Come on Down: LET'S MAKE A DEAL

The OJ verdict was read at 1:30PM EST on Tuesday October 3rd, 1995. No matter your thoughts on justice and the American way, the world thought him guilty. All that remained was the official and legal conclusion of guilt as reached by a jury of his peers and read by a judge.

"NOT-GUILTY!"

The cook screamed out. The counter girls covered their mouths and ran to the front, but their eyes gave them away: Excited shock. The clean-up guy was next to a thrash can, laughing. After all this, the first customer was a White man.

"Can you believe that? Can you believe that guy got off?"

"Can I take your order sir?"

Muhammad spoke clearly as the order girls stood to the side sighing in disbelief.

"They let that guy, that murderer get away. That idiotic jury, what were they thinking?"

"Can I take your order sir?"

"Sheesh...I'll take a number two with a coke"

Soon the store was packed with regular customers who usually came at 12. Seems they put their lunch on hold awaiting the verdict. This was that rare day when food was not the number one subject in a restaurant. OJ, OJ, OJ that was all anyone talked about on this particular afternoon. Even to the end of Muhammad's shift at 6 o'clock all the customers, all the workers had something to say about OJ. Yet, just before CNN made a big deal of it, Muhammad noticed that his White customers were shocked and angry, the Black customers were shocked and excited, or was that happy? For Muhammad, it was just a rich man who got off. And if he had played his cards right he too would be rich.

By time he got home and turned on the cable TV, CNN was replaying over and over again with split screen or in any public place the different racial reactions to the verdict at the instant it was announced...He was right... The race card. There were the commentators saying that this was smart or that that was lucky. They spoke on the future of OJ and the lawyers and the growing potency of "If it don't fit, you must acquit". Then it came out that most of the jurors were minorities. Muhammad could actually see the White commentators seethe...The Black commentators, reporters and office help in the background were all holding back smiles. By midnight they realized that OJ was still up on civil charges and could be tried again for 'wrongful death'. Watching the television Charlie picks up the phone and dials his answering service. He pushed a few bottons and listened as once again CNN showed the split screen reaction.

"As of October 3rd your available balance is...One Thousand, Thirty Two Dollars and Forty Three Cents."

*The Adventures of Muhammad Smith and The Million Man March*

That was up about $300 since he last checked two days ago. Maybe eight tickets, not even enough to fill a bus. Almost every channel on TV was talking about the verdict. He glanced at the bag of weed Stevie had given him but then glanced back at the TV: OJ, OJ, OJ. Carm was a Sunday thing, his friends left him with his last real job. The crew at the Fast Food Delite only knew him as the boss and Abraham was in a Alabama jail. It was no secret that Muhammad was alone. With the world abuzz with OJ and his bank account showing the promise of a future, there was no one to talk to.

He called the service one last time before he fell asleep..."One Thousand, Seventy Two Dollars and Forty Three Cents."

One ticket, Whipity do.

7:30AM the alarm radio went off to KYW, news radio. The subject: Traffic, weather and OJ. Rubbing his eyes to the stark apartment he turned off the radio and clicked on the TV. Again OJ. He did the toilet stoop, the face shave and the morning shower. From his chair he grabbed his Fast Food Delite uniform placed there the night before. With routine effort he put his uniform on and grabbed the phone, dialed the number, a few buttons and he listened...

"Two Thousand, Two Hundred, Forty Two Dollars and Forty Three Cents."

That woke him up.

********

Raheem was all that. Straight A's from Kindergarten to his current University of

Pennsylvania pre-med school. Staying in Philly to be a part of his Mother's organization. Even at the age of 20 he was the strongest man at the Inner-city Society for the Improvement of Sisterhood. Where he failed at Basketball, he excelled at piano; Jazz, Classic, Motown, The Beatles. Raised by his Grandparents and loved by his mother, Raheem, complete with dread locks, was on his way. In his last year of pre-med school it was already known that he would be an intern by the age of 23, a young doctor. Everyone was proud of him, even Muhammad. But Muhammad himself had no children. To Raheem he was just Mr. Smith, some guy his mother knew. It was Thursday morning, two days after the verdict and there at Broad and Chestnut Streets Raheem saw Charlie.

"Good morning Mr. Smith."

"Raheem! College boy and High School Graduate. What's up?"

"Just going to my mother's office. They need help over there on the phones. All of a sudden everyone wants to go to the Million Man March."

"Well imagine that."

"They're talking about organizing some trips. Hey Mr. Smith I have to go. Take care."

Dashing across Broad Street he screams…

"I'll tell my mom I saw you."

Charlie smiled at the thought. He then quickly turned his attention through the doors of the Land Title Building of 100 South Broad Street. If luck is when preparation meets opportunity, then it was Charlie's lucky day. Before Tuesday he had wasted almost $100,000. On Tuesday he realized it was well spent. He had his 400 buses spread from Newark

New Jersey to The heart of the south in Atlanta. The posters he insisted on, the answering service he hired complete with a pay by phone option. The 800 number made it so much the better. By time he woke up this Thursday morning his account had grown by $20,000 in little more than two days.

These people from 'The Land Title building' who called him last night called themselves the Mercury Bus Corporation. If this was the Mercury Bus Company that he knew, it was a first class organization, was around for about 50 years and had some of the prettiest buses on the road. They said they had heard he was renting buses and that perhaps they could strike a deal. He told them he had about as much as he could handle plus their prices were too high. They said that he had picked a good day, October the 16$^{th}$. No school trips, families tied down after a summer of spending and old folks with monthly checks, stuck in the middle of the month. Charlie was slightly surprised that they knew nothing of the Million Man March. Before the OJ verdict it was just a subject to pass time and in the White community it wasn't even on the radar. As CNN flashed split screen images of the Black and White reactions to the verdict, a groundswell took hold in Black America. It was good that the Mercury Bus Corporation didn't know about the Million Man March. After all this was a Black thing.

It was the typical conference room with long table and cute swivel chairs. He sat at the end furthest from the door the receptionist had walked him through. Then he waited, a short while…

*Anonymous*

"Mr. Smith, hello I'm Walter Peters, general manger of Mercury Bus Corp."

He was a middle aged man with the prerequisite suit and tie followed into the room by a big and burly Black guy, who looked more like a body guard than the admin type. Regardless he was dressed the same way as the middle aged guy. Charlie stood in his blue jeans and blazer.

"Mr. Peters, a pleasure to meet you."
"Please Mr. Smith have a seat."
The three of them sat with Peters keeping an eye on the relaxing Muhammad. They looked to each other with a smile.
"Mr. Smith you've been spending a lot of cash money for buses."
"How would you know that Mr. Peters?"
"Mr. Smith, I'm in the bus business. I get paid to know the bus business. This 'million man' thing...
Now he had Charlie's attention.
"...may work out but the NAACP and the Rainbow Coalition want no part of it. What makes you so certain that anybody will go?"
Measuring every word
"Well...Mr. Peters, fact of the matter is I'll probably lose all or most of my money. What makes you so interested?"
"Fact of the matter is Mr. Smith is that you've collected at least ten thousand dollars since Tuesday and chances are that by next Tuesday you'll have made all of your money back and by this time next

*The Adventures of Muhammad Smith and The Million Man March*

week you'll be spending your first profit. Probably the first profit you've ever earned in your whole life Mr. Smith, or at least since you began work at Fast Food Delite."

"Excuse me! Excuse me if I'm rude but where do you get off telling me about my life and if I'm making all this money then why ain't you out there raking in the bucks?"

"Mr. Smith I've told you my business is the bus business and when a young man such as yourself goes up and down the east coast buying up all the independents for one day, and of all days a Monday, we make a point to know where he drives his Cadillac on a Sunday night. We make it a point to call your apartment Mr. Smith two minutes after you walk through the front door."

"OK, Mr...Walters, this meeting is over. We have nothing to talk about."

Charlie gets up to leave.

"Mr. Smith we are prepared to offer our fleet of one thousand buses, maybe more, for a price of three hundred fifty dollars per bus per day, plus $50 for insurance. Our buses can be anywhere in the country with 24 hours notice and we can help you with your whole operation."

Charlie stops when he hears this and turns.

"If you got me all figured out then why ain't you selling tickets to the Million Man March?"

"This may come as a surprise to you but I'm not Black."

"No, it's no surprise at all Mr. Walters. But we don't have nothing to talk about Mr. Walters. I got enough buses and even if I did want more buses I ain't payin' your inflated rates. So really, this conversation is over."

He then proceeded on.

"A national fleet Mr. Smith for your Black, feel good, *give a buck for the cause,* get-together. You're a smart man. Figure it out...LA will pay perhaps a hundred, perhaps a hundred fifty per seat. But they can't travel that distance in the rinky dink buses you have Mr. Smith."

"I don't get the Sunday night, Cadillac part."

"We don't care if you sleep with White women Mr. Smith. Really we don't even like your Cadillac..."

"You White Racist..."

The burly Black guy merely stood up. Charlie took notice.

"Oh, so it's like that hunh."

"We just need a Black face Mr. Smith and actually we do like your operation, the way you use the phones...Direct payment, 800 number...cute. You want to go to listen to somebody call me a racist you go right ahead, just use the services of my company...that's all...It's win, win Mr. Smith."

"And if I don't then John Henry here gonna like follow me to the parking lot...What's going on, is this a mafia thing, a stick up thing. And How Come You Got This Monkey Lookin..,Ape lookin at ME.?"

Peters gives the man a look with a nod and the big Black guy leaves the room...

"First of all Mr. Smith my name is Walter Peters, so please call me Mr. Peters. Second of all let's wipe the slate clean. I need a Black face to do business for me. In this land where not a soul is racist, a million black men are indeed going to Washington, I believe

*The Adventures of Muhammad Smith and The Million Man March*

that. But I'm not putting a White driver on that bus, not a White driver who works for a White man. I need somebody Black, Mr. Smith."

"So what's wrong with the doofus who just left the room?"

Smiling..."You can actually read and write at a 12$^{th}$ grade level Mr. Smith, that's not a common thing. But beyond that you've actually put together a solid organization...cute."

"You like this word, 'cute'?"

"No Mister Smith that is not the cutest word. The cutest word is 'Muhammad'. "

"What does that mean?"

"It means that I need a Black face, I don't trust these Muslims. I don't want to deal with them. But by time everybody figures out that they're pissed off and want to go see somebody call me a pig, by time they figure that out It'll be to late to make the plans to go. We need them to commit now Mr. Smith and you are ready now."

"You know I don't like this whole spy and race thing."

"You know while the rest of the world can clearly see it, no one in America, not one soul respected outside of their neighborhood has ever admitted that they were racist. Did you know that little tidbit of history Mr. Smith? No one White and *of course* no one Black...No one admits to being 'Racist' ". He looks to Charlie for a response. "You know Mr. Smith my grandfather thinks you're little more than a dog."

"And what do you think Mr. Peters?"

"Well, do monkeys count?"

*Anonymous*

"HA!"

Muhammad was loud but pure. Maybe he wanted to drown it out. Walter didn't blink an eye. He was serious.

"You're serious aren't you?"

"Let's just say that monkeys don't get enough credit."

"I can't believe you would say such nonsense." He put his hands to his Jerry curled head. "And I'm thinkin' about doing business with you?"

"Do you like Rock and Roll Mr. Smith, not the Lynard Synard kind but the 1950's kind? People like Authur Alexander and "Anna, Go to Him" or maybe Gene Allison's "You Can Make it if You Try". Have you ever heard of them Mr. Smith? Or has Elvis Presley completely blinded your eyes?"

"Man what are you talking about?"

"Mr. Smith on occasion I've had the opportunity to hear people like Malcolm X, Elijah Muhammad and the honorable Louis Farrakhan. Do you know what Thurgood Marshall said about the Black Muslim's Mr. Smith?"

"You know Mr. Peters, I don't see where's that's any of your business."

"Mr. Muhammad Charles Smith of the Second Street AME Church I'm about to make you a millionaire and elevate you from the joys of Fast Food Delite. I'm trying to help you here Mr. Smith."

"OK. So offer me a contract and I'll think about it."

"Why do you think I'm offering this to you Mr. Smith? I mean really I could find anyone."

*The Adventures of Muhammad Smith and The Million Man March*

"But I got the operation. I mean it's like you said the 800 number, the direct pay."

Peters taps the table top.

"We have 800 numbers and direct pay and dial up computer access, we don't need your stinking operation. What I need Mr. Smith is a black face to go to Washington and tell America to wake up." He stands. "I don't know why you started buying up buses two weeks ago but I suspect it's because you're one of the few Americans who realizes that everybody's pissed off. There are issues here that are separating neighbor against neighbor, father against son, Black against White...husband against wife. I control a national fleet of buses Mr. Smith and I want a million men to be in Washington for my own selfish reasons."

"You got issues Mr. Peters. Maybe I can use your buses but this Black face jazz scares me. Just show me the contract man."

Walter took his measure of Muhammad.

"Follow me to my office Mr. Smith, or is it Muhammad?"

"Go on."

Charlie followed Mr. Peters down the hall to a rather large office on the corner of the floor. Going into the office Walter offered Charlie a seat facing his desk. Above the desk was a picture up on the wall. It was a picture from the 40's, with a GI in dress uniform, his wife and obviously their child who obviously was Walter Peters. Other than that the GI was Black and the woman was White. The parents of our Mr. Peters, Charlie thought? And there on the desk was the General Manager himself in what appeared to be a family picture. In the picture Walter stands next to a woman of his age...a woman who is Black. Surrounding him and this woman in the picture were three other, younger couples, who in turn stood next to children. In this picture stood everything from blue eyed Blond to stone cold Black. Muhammad looked studiously to Walter who was taking his seat.

"Do you like my pictures Mr. Smith?"

"Interesting."

Walter smiles.

"I was born and raised in England Mr. Smith, don't let my accent fool you. I see America quite differently than you."

"How so is that Mr. Peters?"

"Everything about this bloody country is racist from the Debutants in Haddon Heights to the Niggers in North Philly."

There was that word. Whenever a White person said that word, in any scenario, it simply hit his ear as 'sub-human species'...A sub human species in the grand order of things. But yet once when he was robbed at gunpoint and he heard 'Nigger give me the money' the word seemed to calm him...as if the grit and grime of everyday life. But right now things weren't so Black and White.

"Buddy, I don't get it. You want a million black people to go to DC? To prove what? I mean why is it a big deal to you?"

"Look at your hair Mr. Smith. They call that a 'Jerry Curl" don't they?"

"Mr. Peters, I haven't connected two dots since I got here."

Walter sighed in humor.

"Here's your contract, signed along with a copy…It's not complicated Mr. Smith, our standard form in fact. We don't organize events we only rent to organizers. I think you'll find it very fair. Take a day to read it but make your mind up by tomorrow. When my bosses discover this million man march I'm sure we'll be banned from doing business. I need that contract Mr. Smith. I believe our business for the day is over…Robert," Walter intercommed for his assistant "…could you show Mr. Smith to the door." Promptly the big burly Black guy walked into the office. "Mr. Smith meet doofus, my grandson Robert Prescott Peters."

Charlie smiled with contract in hand and rose.

"Mr. Peters I'm not sure but I think I like you."

"Good, you'll make a good customer."

Peters looked through him as he smiled. Charlie whimpered a smile and turned to leave…

"Mr. Smith, as long as you allow yourself to be measured on the yardstick of silky hair, you'll never measure up. Perhaps Farrakhan will tell you that you are more than a victim."

Charlie returned a short smile and left. This Million Man thing was getting complicated.

********

Raheem arrived at his mother's office. The national headquarters of the Inner-city Society for the Improvement of Sisterhood, or ISIS as his Mother the founder liked to call it. She claimed it was Egyptian and thus, by default it was Black. Raheem knew that

*Anonymous*

his fellow students from northern Africa did not claim to be Black. And the few who could, on a bad day, pass for Black had no clue why he was wearing dreadlocks in his hair. Raheem had a completely different view of White Men than his mother. After all half of her membership was lesbian.

"Hi Mom"

"Good morning Raheem."

"I saw Mr. Smith today, just a few minutes ago at Broad and Chestnut."

She kept typing.

"And?..."

"Nothing I just saw Mr. Smith that's all. So you want me to grab one of these phones."

"Yes, this Million Man thing is getting complicated. People want to go but we can't find any buses. She typed and read, and corrected various papers and screens on her desk. Raheem leaned against the wall wondering.

"Mom?"

"Yes Raheem!?"

"Grandpop says Mr. Smith could have been my daddy. What does that mean?"

Finally she stopped typing.

"Raheem we've talked about this before. I told you me and Mr. Smith used to be friends that's all"

"Oh. Well I'm going to pick up a phone now. Take care mom."

"Take care Raheem."

Once he left she sat back looking off into space. Seemingly focused on some vague memory from long ago.

"Miss Morgan, you have the Rainbow Coalition on line five."

The PA system awoke her from her dream... That's all it was, a dream.

# The Fun Begins: PEE WEE's PLAYHOUSE

Pee Wee had no last name. He was merely a ten year old child who never knew his father, biological or other wise. At a little before two in the morning he sat in his ramshackle room mesmerized by what he held in his hands. His mother was a crack head who had just entered the front door of their disheveled, dirty and filthy home. She hadn't bathed in three days and the dress she wore betrayed her stick figure legs. The man who followed her in was little more than a junkie himself, dressed in torn blue jeans and a hooded sweat shirt. His reaction to the thrash that surrounded him was hidden behind the hood that covered his face. She motioned for him to wait as she walked to the stairs.

"Pee Wee?"

He heard her but chose not to answer. Something in his view held his attention as he sat on the mattress which lay on the floor amidst plastic bags of trash and clothes.

"PEE WEE?"

"Yeah ma."

"What you doin' boy?"

*The Adventures of Muhammad Smith and The Million Man March*

"I'm looking at TV."

Of course the broken TV screen made this an obvious lie…But who cared?

"Mom, you got any food, I'm hungry?"

Perhaps looking for dinner, maybe more.

"Go to bed boy. I'll get some Corn Flakes in the mornin'"

"With milk this time Ma?"

"I said go to bed boy!"

It was all so routine. She grabbed the strangers hand to the couch in the next room. She lifted the trash bag from the couch and three mice scattered about. The stranger sat. She kneeled before him grabbing the five dollars placed suddenly in front of her and with a few short movements and the sound of a zipper her head disappeared into the strangers lap. Upstairs Pee Wee's eyes looked up as if to dream of all that could be. He leaned over to turn on the radio. Against the dirty white sheet his right hand pressed into the mattress and the nickel plated pistol carelessly made it's impression into the bed. The station was the routine…'DAS. The music was the Spinners.

The gun was loaded.

********

"Hey man you know a small kid who be out here at like three in the morning? Sucker got my gun."

They stood on the corner of 63rd and Filbert, just outside the Korean Deli, just a little before 2AM, in the heart of what suburbia knew as the ghetto. But these two men were quite comfortable.

"Your gun!? Gee boss, how that happen?"

"Cops pulled me over and I tossed it. Then I see this midget kid grab my piece and I can't do nothing...Cop got me pulled over."

"Man it be kids out all times of night. Half these women on that pipe. You know how that go Gee."

"Yeah, yeah never mind all that, how many pounds you do today

"I don't know, maybe three. Maybe six. I ain't heard from 46$^{th}$ street yet."

"How many grams."

"Oh we did about half a key of coke."

"Where's the money."

"At the cleaners like you said."

"Alright, good, good"

They sipped at coffee as all was understood.

"Listen you see some crumb snatcher yappin' about a gun you let me know...As a matter fact let the kid know too."

"OK Steve."

"I'm out."

*********

Charlie had to know...His academic curiosity was peeked. What did Thurgood Marshall say about the Muslims? Thurgood Marshall was that rare entity, a Black academic who held universal respect through the whole Black population as well as every White lawyer who opposed him in court. Appointed to the Supreme Court by LBJ and the first Black to sit on the court. Ebony Magazine did a few page fives on him. Just what did Thurgood say about the Muslims? The proud, bow tied, veiled Muslims. Just how does one go

*The Adventures of Muhammad Smith and The Million Man March*

about finding such information in 1995? At the library he looked in the indexes of several biographies of the famed Judge. Charlie didn't find 'Muslim' in any of the books but in one he found 'Muhammad, Elijah..., Pg 128'. But that was only a phrase that said Thurgood equaled in stature the respect given to all the leaders of the day to include Phillip Randolph, Elijah Muhammad and several others. Still from this he looked at the index of the one biography he found on Elijah Muhammad. Nothing. Still the word "Obituary" caught Charlie's eye. On a hunch he went to the librarian and asked if there was an index for obituaries in the New York Times.

"What Year?"

Charlie was clueless.

"Do you have a name?"

He told her Thurgood Marshall..."And Elijah Muhammad too."

Thurgood's Obituary, less than two years old was the routine...Still his was an outstanding profile. Born to the Colored middle class of Baltimore, Maryland in 1908. His mother was a teacher for Colored children, his daddy a butler. He worked his way through to be first in his class at Howard University in 1933 and then on to Brown Vs The Board of Education in 1954. Then when affirmative action came into play, he had a front row seat. Why even Kennedy said "He's argued 32 cases in front of the Supreme Court and he's won 29 of them. If that's not a qualification for the Supreme Court then I am not an American." In 1967, LBJ made that qualification a reality. And there sat Thurgood Marshall, of the Supreme Court of the United States of America. The obituary went on to read that he was a great father and loving husband who died in 1993 but nothing about the Muslims. Charlie then turned to Elijah Muhammad.

> Elijah Muhammad Dead: Black Muslim Leader, 77...Chicago, Feb. 25, 1975...Born 1897...Elijah Poole...Georgia, Detroit, Chicago, 1942, Michigan...COMMENTS By MARSHALL.

'Bingo' Charlie's mind lit up, finally...What Marshall...,

> 'a Black liberal', said...1959..."run by a bunch of thugs organized from prisons and jails and financed, I am sure, by Nasser or some Arab group." Marshall added that followers of Mr. Muhammad were "vicious" and a threat to the FBI.

Charlie had often thought such things but he never spoke such things. In the world that he grew in, such things were never said. If anything was said it was more akin to the next paragraph in the New York Times obituary.

> ...a Black conservative, George Schuyler... in 1959...held the view more common to many among the Black masses..."Mr. Muhammad may be a rogue and a charlatan, but when anybody can get tens of thousands of Negroes to practice economic solidarity, respect their women, alter their atrocious diet, give up liquor,

stop crime, juvenile delinquency and adultery, he is doing more for Negroes' welfare than any current Negro leader I know."

Charlie collected his thoughts and left the Library into the midday sun. For the first time he really gave pause to just what would the Minister Farrakhan say to a mass of Black men pissed off because the White Man don't even like OJ Simpson: Would it be vicious or solidarity.

********

Pee Wee tip-toed down the steps, sure that his mother was sleep. Sure enough she lay in the lap of some hooded stranger, in a pile of trash with a pipe in her hand. Pee Wee could only look. Then as the clock radio showed 2:08 AM he turned and left to the brisk October night. Soon he would find his way to Filbert Street.

Bobby was Stevie's ace boon coon and everyone on 63rd Street knew it. His reputation alone kept a lot of nonsense away. Sure Filbert Street was the wrong place to be at 2AM in the ghetto. But this was where his car was parked and anyone who knew that two plus two was four, knew not to give Bobby any nonsense, static or trouble.

Pee Wee, who had flunked his math test earlier in the day, saw the man turn onto Filbert from the other end and he just made up his mind to do it. He kept walking toward this stranger feeling bolder with each step with the feel of what he held in his right coat pocket.

Bobby saw the figure down the street and knew straight off that it was a child. His mind just as quickly

*Anonymous*

turned to another thought, it had been a long day. Getting to his Silver Shadow Mercedes Benz he pushed the remote lock. The lights flashed, the horn beeped.

Pee Wee saw the gray car beep. Still he walked towards this man and pulled the gun out of his coat pocket. Bobby noticed that the kid had picked up his pace a bit but the closer the child got to him the more obvious it was that it was just a harmless kid. He didn't notice when this child held up his right arm. When Pee Wee saw that this man was looking at him his instinct hastened his pace. Bobby took a second, good look…That's when he saw the gun.

"Stick up mister."

He was caught off guard but still cracked a smile… This was a kid, a short, midget kid.

"Man what do you want?"

"Give me your money mister. I mean it."

Bobby slowly reached into his pocket and shed a twenty off of his pile of 20's, 50's and 100's.

"Here kid..."

Pee Wee cautiously grabbed the twenty from the giving and smiling Bobby and turned to run…

"Now you can get your mom some crack."

Something overcame Pee Wee. He turned and instantly shot off three rounds from the gun. With the same speed the surprising recoil knocked him to the ground in a blaze of gunfire. Still he shuffled back to his feet to see this stranger laying on the ground with blood running over his open eyes. Shocked for a moment Pee Wee ran to this dead man, grabbed one pocket full of money and ran.

\*\*\*\*\*\*\*\*

With the pay phone held loosely to his ear, he wanted to hear this again.

"Twenty Eight Thousand, Four Hundred Thirty Nine Dollars and Seventeen Cents"

"I'M NIGGER RICH!!!"

He screamed. The White couple nearby stepped across the street, tourists probably. Charlie could only smile at the sight of them. Twenty nine grand, he was rich. Why that and some good credit, he could buy anything. He figured his first payment would be on his seven credit cards, on two of them he was late. This was it. Nobody could get in his way. Just that morning he was only at twenty thousand. Now four hours later, just out of the library, another nine thousand dollars materialized out of nowhere. He looked at the contract that this guy, Walter Peters, had given him. He didn't like the price at $400.00 per day per bus, but what the heck, he was nigger rich…, money didn't matter. Later that day he made the minimum credit card payment. But first he walked back to Broad Street to the Land Title Building. He signed the contract and left it with the receptionist. He wasn't obligated unless he ordered a bus, cash on demand. Mercury was obligated to rent to him for the seven days from October 13th to October 19th. It was only Thursday, but Chuckie wanted to see Carmillia. He called her office.

"Carm? Carm, it's me Chuckie. I feelin' good baby how about you?"

"Chuckie, I'm at work. You know I can't take calls. For Christ sake Chuckie, I'm at the front desk."

"Tonight, baby, tonight…Let's do the "Le Bec Fin" thing. South Street, Walnut Street…Your call baby."

*Anonymous*

"Chuckie you know my week nights are busy. Besides I'm going to the OJ protest at City Hall. Chuckie, you should really come and show your support."

"Support, support for what?"

"Chuckie that was a travesty what happened in that courtroom and you know it."

"Look Carm, I just want to go out, get some good food, some good everything. Come on babe, we never go…"

"Chuckie it's Mr. Goldberg! I have to go."

That was a bummer. But not to worry, he had tickets to mail, plans to make and bills to pay. He made his way to the answering service he had hired on the second floor of a small building at 13th and Sansom. He smiled at the clerk, waited for the list. From here he drove home to West Philly and got the roll of tickets he printed up. He put an extra fifty dollars in it to make them fancy.

## ROUND TRIP FARE TO
## THE MILLION MAN MARCH
## OCTOBER 16, 1995
*Charles, Muhammad Enterprises Inc.*

He drove his Cadillac to the post office at 63rd and Master. Envelopes, stamps and to his surprise, more than an hour addressing them, complete with his return PO Box address. He was going to have to do better than this. Then he went to the bank, a withdraw for five thousand, eight hundred ninety two dollars and fifty three cents. He couldn't resist when the teller asked if he wanted his balance.

"Yes mam."

*The Adventures of Muhammad Smith and The Million Man March*

She perked her eye, smiled at Muhammad.

"Here you are Mister Smith."

The piece of paper sat atop the pile of hundred dollar bills and the teller was still smiling. Charlie stuck the pile in his pocket and glanced at the paper...$32, 719.17.

"Thank you mam."

Now she was looking into his eyes with the same smile.

"Thank You Mister Smith."

He could get use to this 'Mr. Smith' thing. He walked away with a jaunt in his step, a certain rhythm. It was something like that George and Weezie song, as best as Charlie could remember it...

Well we movin on up

To the east side

To a deluxe, duplex complex in the sky..

Yeah we movin' on up

To the west side

I finally got a piece of the pie.

He went shopping for a suit at Boyds, brought jewelry at Baily, Banks and Briddle and ate a 10 dollar hamburger at Baines on Broad Street. Then Muhammad goes to a barber shop at Germantown and Lehigh Avenues.

"Hey Charlie, where you been nigger and what's that concoction on your head."

"Oh this?"

He rubs his Jerry Curl.

"Well Mr. Al I was hopin' you could help me with that."

*Anonymous*

"Com'on get your butt in this chair boy before I throw a meat cleaver and whack that there creation off your head."

The two old men playing checkers laughed. It was the end of the jerry curl. After all, Michael Jackson was getting old.

Next stop was the printer. He had ordered posters for Pittsburgh, the farthest west he had gone. His last city. He had only signed the contract, via fax, on Monday morning. A day before everything had changed. He was particularly proud of the poster: The welcoming Black hands extending from a glow over a mass of Black men.

## BLACK MAN
## PILGRIMAGE OF FAITH
## THE MILLION MAN MARCH

It was complete with his 800 number and the location for the bus to pick people up. The same as all his posters in Newark, NJ, Newark, Delaware, Chester, PA and in New York City. But for each city the pick up point had to be changed. No biggie…What was a biggie was that today was a sick day. Tomorrow he had to work at Fast Food Delite.

## Have it Your Way: BURGER KING

"May I take your order please?"

The smile was forced. The customer was a middle aged bespectacled white guy with gray hair and a two day worn suit.

"May I have a Whopper please?"

"Sir we don't sell Whoppers. Would you like a Deluxe Delite?"

Charlie was no better with a plaid tie, against a two-tone shirt. Without the Jerry Curl it didn't look right.

The customer was so much the more clueless. Lost at the thought of no Whoppers he blankly looked to Muhammad, who blankly looked back at him. Then with a jerk the white guy looked to the menu.

"Do you have any specials? I have Whopper coupons…Do you take Whopper coupons?"

"Ah, no sir."

The customer went back to the menu.

"Would you like to try our Double Delite sir for a dollar fifty nine."

"Mmmmm….."

"Or you can get a Whopper two blocks down on Broad Street, right next to the Reverend Doctor Martin

Luther King Jr. Rehabilitation Center. You can't miss it sir."

"Mmm, I take two Double Delites, a large fry and a vanilla milk shake."

Charlie gave the customer the eye as he leaned to the mike by the register.

"Two dubs."

Slowly Muhammad turned away from the customer, out of caution, and then snapped to a smile for the next customer.

"May I take your…"

"Could I have one those without cheese?"

The middle aged white guy couldn't get enough. Muhammad darted his eye straight to the guy who's only response was…

"Please."

Muhammad turns…

"Eddie, make one of them dubs without cheese."

"Al'ight"

And then, again, the cautious eye to the white guy

"Will that be all sir?"

"Yes thank you very muc…"

"Your order mam?"

"Mr. Smith, the dubs"

"Thanks Eddie."

Charlie turned for the fries dumping a batch and almost in one motion salted them.

"Ohhh. I'm sorry, I didn't want the salt. You see I'm on a salt diet and my doctor told me no more salt. Thyroids. Sheesh how I could I forget, I'm so sorry."

Muhammad just looked. And then he smiled.

"Yes Sir!"

*The Adventures of Muhammad Smith and The Million Man March*

Charlie hustled into his work, his last day of work. As soon as Mr. Middle Aged White guy left, Charlie called James.

"James man I got some bad news."

"You got robbed."

"No not today. It's something else. I got something cookin' and I gotta go."

"Just ask Aunt Sally to go over and take it off the stove. She still has the key to your apartment doesn't she? I mean after all she owns..."

"No James I'm not cooking I'm quitting."

This was followed by a silence.

"...See Charlie that's your problem, you never finish anything. It was Aunt Sally who made me give you this job. Now just like that you gone. What, what are you going to do? Get a job at Burger King, or Wendy's?"

"James it's nothing like that. It's that bus thing, I think it's going to work."

"You still thinking about that Million Man thing? Aunt Sally is going to want more than your thoughts to pay the rent Charlie. Responsible people realize these things."

"James, I'm leaving. This is my last day of the week anyway. You got Saturday and Sunday to find someone and if this Million Man thing is just a fluke then I'll be back in two weeks."

"Charlie I can't hold this job for you for two weeks."

"That's what I'm tellin' you man, I quit."

Another silence.

"...Can Eddie read?"

"Yeah he reads, maybe 10${}^{th}$ grade level, but he can swing it. He knows the routine and no matter the shift, he's the only one on time. That's a good idea James."

"Does Aunt Sally know that you are quitting?"

"I'll tell her."

"…This Million Man thing hunh?"

"Yep James, the Million Man thing."

"Hmmph."

James hung up.

"HEY EDDIE."

Muhammad was on a roll.

"Yeah Mr. Smith?"

"You know Mr. Brown don't you?"

Writing down James number as he approached Eddie.

"Yeah."

"Here's his number give him a call at lunch time."

"What I do?"

"Eddie, just call…And tell him you want 13 an hour."

Now they were smiling. In fact all the way through the rest of the day until 6 o'clock, that's all it was, a smile.

*********

Friday night and he was home now, alone with his cable and the bag of weed on the table, just next to where he sat. Stevie had given him that bag a little more than a week ago and still he hadn't smoked a lick. There was no particular reason why he wasn't smoking the weed. He just wasn't. About eight days ago he realized that he was getting things done. Often, while high, he thought great thoughts but never did anything. The clapper, that was his idea…but he didn't get a patent. Over the years he often wondered about this, while he was high, of the connection between idleness and being high. Even if the drug, reefer lets say, is physically harmless, the essence of being high was doing nothing.

So now it was him and CNN, post OJ. It was an amazing transfixion for the nation. In all reality the OJ Murder/Trial held a national audience 24 hours a day for almost a whole year, and now it was coming to an end. Johnny Cochran, went from a big shot LA lawyer to a national celebrity. Greta Van Susteren went from an unknown legal analyst to the know all and see all of the trial. In spite of her Annie Oakly looks she made more sense than anybody else. Not only did Television elevate it's stature, but whole industries of T-Shirts and books and White Ford Broncos arose overnight and made dozens millionaires. Now Charlie watched as the TV spoke of the OJ murder, trial and verdict. Every channel played it's own thick and somber music.

DUNH-DUNH-DUNH-DA-DA-DUNH-DUNH-
DUNH-DA-DA.
**VERDICT ON TRIAL**

Then, just before he fell asleep he saw Bernard Shaw on CNN mention…

"Louis Farrakhan, is a Minister from Chicago. A majority of Americans have never heard of him. But a minority of Americans know him intimately."

They cut to film, it's a clip of Malcolm X giving a firery speech from the 50's.

"The American Negro did not land on Plymouth Rock, Plymouth Rock landed on him."

Bernard Shaw takes the camera again.

"They're known as the Black Muslims, though they call themselves the Nation of Islam. Their members have included the well spoken Malcolm X and the loud speaker Muhammad Ali, who is no longer with the group. A Black nationalist group with roots going back to the 30's in Detroit, Michigan and Chicago, Illinois which is where we find Minster Louis Farrakhan. No we can't interview Mr. Farrakhan. Except for these few file photos we'll have to wait and see Mr. Farrakhan on his terms, which just so happens to be about a week from now when he's planning to hold a 'million man march' at the Mall in Washington DC."

Jeff Greenfeld the reporter cut in.

"It's my understanding that, if this were to occur, it would be the first such million person protest."

Right then Muhammad knew he sold 40 buses.

"I understand they're calling it a 'Day of Atonement'"

"But why do you need a million Black men to 'Atone'"

"Well he's holding the rally two Mondays from today on the Mall in Washington DC."

"Well he picked a bad time with America… transfixed by this OJ thing."

"Jeff, you may well be right."

Then the OJ music….

DUNH-DUNH-DUNH-DA-DA-DUNH-DUNH-DUNH-DA-DA

*The Adventures of Muhammad Smith and The Million Man March*

"And when we return we'll have our special report on 'Juries Run Amok'".

Through the commercial for Hertz Rent-a-Car Muhammad thought to call for one last check to his bank account. He hadn't checked it all day. The totals were starting to scare him. He planned this much money, but he never knew this much money. First he had to pay his grandmother off. The buses were already paid for. Soon it would be all profit. Four hundred buses, more than three hundred thousand dollars pure profit. Even as he fell asleep, Muhammad still had a smile on his face.

Saturday morning came with a bang. The answering service called. There was a problem. Someone in Pittsburgh had purchased tickets for four hundred Black Boy Scouts and wanted to know if each bus had a chaperone. It was 9:30 on a Saturday morning and Charlie didn't have a clue.

"Tell them, I'll get back to 'em."

"OK Mr. Smith but they are very persistant."

"OK, OK let me think, I'll call you back. I promise I'll call back."

Now what? A chaperone for every bus...four hundred tickets...about 10 grand...Now what?

Charlie fell back on the bed covering his eyes and said...

"Now what?"

Then he dropped his hand with focused eyes. With receiver still in hand he sat up and dialed a number.

"Hello, hello Mrs. Morgan is that you?"

"Yes, who am I talking to."

*Anonymous*

"Mrs. Morgan it's me Muhammad from Jenks Elementary."

"Muhammad is that you? Why I haven't spoken to you in years. How you been boy?"

"I'm fine and yourself?"

"Oh I'm getting along. But not like I use to when I was a whipper snapper."

"Ah you're still young Mrs. Morgan. Kept the old phone number I see."

"You know I was never one for all this modern technology Muhammad."

"I remember Mrs. Morgan. How's Mr. Morgan?"

"…Oh he passed three years ago. But I'm fine, I'm fine."

"I was hoping I could find Stephanie over there."

"That girl got her own house now over in Mount Airy. I don't know what she be doing these days. I ain't seen her with a man since that professor fella told her he was married. Yeah, I'm sure she'd like to hear from you Muhammad."

"Naw Mrs. Morgan, you don't understand it's just that I need some help with some buses, that's all."

"You got a pen and paper Muhammad. Let me give you this number and y'all can bus that stuff all over the city."

He wrote it down laughing at her innuendo.

"Thank you Mrs. Morgan."

"Now you tell her that her mother sent you and you don't take no mess. You hear me Muhammad?"

"OK Mrs. Morgan…Thank you Mrs. Morgan…Yes I will stop by for some of your bean pie Mrs. Morgan… OK, goodbye."

Hanging up there was a short hesitation.

*The Adventures of Muhammad Smith and The Million Man March*

In Mount Airy there was a quick answer.

"Hello…Is this Stephanie?"

"No she's in the bedroom I'll get her."

It was a woman's voice but it wasn't Stephanie.

"Hello, This is Ms. Morgan. Who is this?"

"Stephanie good morning. It's me Muhammad."

"Muhammad, how did you get my number?"

"Oh, I see. Listen Steph I apologize for calling you on a Saturday morning. It was only business anyway, so I'll stop by your office on Monday. OK?"

There was silence…A fairly long silence.

"Is this about Stevie Muhammad? You know I didn't like that right?"

"OK I can be sloppy sometime. But no this ain't about nobody. Just business."

"Muhammad, what business could a North American, Fast Food Delite Negro be about early on a Saturday morning?"

"Wow, so it gotta be like that?"

"I'm listening Muhammad."

"The Million Man March."

"So, you're going to the Million Man March…Since when? Since the verdict?"

"Since a month ago."

"Humph."

"Stephanie I need help. I need help in Pittsburgh. You got offices in Pittsburgh, don't you?"

"No but we work with NOW, United Food and Labor, National Council of Negro Women. I mean, that's one thing we do have, we do have phone numbers. But why is this so important now, on a Saturday."

"I got buses Stephanie. I got more buses than I know what to do with and I can get a thousand more."

"Muhammad by time you call the bus company those buses are going to be gone."

"You're right they are gone and I got 'em. I started renting the buses a month ago just for the one day October the 16th. I'm renting them out for forty dollars a seat."

"Are you the guy who got them Black pilgrimage signs all over town?"

"I'm the guy."

"So where does Pittsburgh come into the picture?"

"I got buses in Pittsburgh too. But I need chaperones for four hundred Black Boy Scouts."

"So you're gonna charge Boy Scouts forty dollars?"

"The tickets are already sold. I told you this was business."

"I see…In fact Muhammad a lot of people are looking for buses, as far away as LA. Like I told you I got the numbers."

"I got the buses."

"STEPHANIE?" It was Joanne from the other room, her roommate. "HAVE YOU SEEN MY UNDERWEAR?"

"IN A MINUTE JOE. Muhammad give me your number. I'll let you know something tomorrow."

"OK, call me."

And, then she slowly says.

"Take care Muhammad"

"Call me Steph."

She hung up.

# Here We Come: The MONKEES

"Strange"

He sprang from bed dressed in the usual Jeans/ Khaki pants with blazer and a sweater if cold. The 'shoes' were canvas Chuck Taylor sneakers. It was an old habit, for luck.

First stop was a plane ride to Pittsburgh. Yes Pittsburgh and Philly are in the same state but Pittsburgh is almost 700 miles away. New York is closer. If he was going to get these posters to Pittsburgh and up on some telephone poles he had to fly. Even though at this point the buses seemed to be selling themselves. Still he wanted to get a lay of the city. Check out the parking lot where all the buses would leave from. Talk face to face with the bus owners. He had asked Carm to come but as always she was busy. It would have been nice to see the sights with her, but Sunday was tomorrow. There would be plenty of time for the old routine on Sunday.

So with $3,000 cash in his pocket he took the subway and then the commuter line to the airport. Check in, seat assignment, padded plastic chairs in the waiting room, a slow moving line, finally after two hours the assigned seat on an airplane. The arrival was the same but faster…Only a crowd to deal with now. Breaking from the crowd he followed the signs to the rent-a-car section and went through the motions until they gave him the map. He literally held it upside down until the rental clerk turned it right side up. This was going to be impossible. His fault though for renting buses at the last minute. In other cities he paid the printers to distribute the posters, but the original Pittsburgh printer ripped him off for the fifty dollar deposit. So he printed them in Philly and now he had to do his own distribution… Simple.

An hour later when he saw the "Come Back To Pittsburgh" sign he figured that he was lost. So he got off at the next exit and turned around. The first familiar thing he saw was the exit sign that read "Martin Luther King Boulevard". He figured he would stop in at a store and ask where the heck he was, besides what better place to hang his signs than "Martin Luther King Blvd".

He turned at the first red light onto the boulevard. Right away it was the ghetto. The homes were decimated. Each block held several empty lots but still had it's contingent of corner boys on the corner. There was a store but Charlie wasn't stopping anywhere near here. There were older men, not old so much as they were dirty. These men were huddled around a fire in a 50 gallon drum even though it wasn't particularly cold. It was late afternoon. There were children playing up and down the street. There were mothers and grandmothers sitting on and standing near the steps of their homes. Just talking, laughing. Muhammad started to feel at ease. He pulled to what appeared to be a major street

*The Adventures of Muhammad Smith and The Million Man March*

with stores. He parks his rent-a-car and walks into a card store...A nice Black shop, apparently.

The music was Marvin Gaye with a picture of Web Dubois on one wall and John Henry on the other. Behind the counter at the front was an older, dignified Black Man. Much what he supposed Mr. Morgan would look like if he were still alive. Complete with gray sweater the old man spoke.

"Yes sir, how can I help you?"

"I'm from out of town and I'm..."

"STICK UP! STICK UP OLD MAN."

It was a kid. A kid, no more than 10 or 12. A kid with a gun.

The old man suddenly got pensive, coiled. The child walked quickly, almost running to the register.

"BACK OFF OLD MAN."

In all truth Muhammad was frozen. The kid had a big, ugly, black gun. Then from the door...

"Hurry up man!"

Another kid, the lookout.

"WHAT YOU LOOKING AT MISTER?"

Charlie could only look away. Still with every corner in his eyeball he looked at that gun, holding his hands out to his side. The old man was pensive, coiled. He slowly moved back.

"Come on old man, I gotta go."

The man stepped back looking at the child's every move, his arm slightly hugging the left side of his gray sweater. The child, his eye's barely reaching the register banged on the buttons but it wouldn't open. The door again.

"Come on Mikey man let's go."

"OPEN THE REGISTER. NOW!!!"

He stretched his arm directly to the old man, gun in hand.

"Open it. OPEN IT NOW!"

The man approached the register, cautiously.

"Come on man."

The child turned for a second to the door.

The old man motioned for his left side.

Just as quick the nervous child jerked back to the old man.

"Open it or I kill you."

Muhammad turned just a bit.

"WHAT YOU LOOKIN FOR MISTER?"

For that second the scared little boy kid turned with gun. The old man pulled out an even bigger gun and got off a shot. He missed. The kid turns and pops the old man with a shot in the stomach and one in the chest. He falls. The kid just runs.

"Agggouuw! Ahhhhgggh."

The old man was definitely shot but with a pain of determination he used every once of his strength, dragging his arm against the floor and with bad aim and a shakey hand he pointed the gun and got the kid as he reached the door.

In the head, square.

His body flew about three feet and then he fell like rocks, he dropped. The kid was dead and the old man was dying. Muhammad sat down right there on the floor right where he stood.

Eight minutes later this is where the cops found him.

********

*The Adventures of Muhammad Smith and The Million Man March*

Seven hundred miles away on Filbert Street, Bobby was forgotten. He was found with his Rolex watch but his pockets were empty. The cops concluded a junkie shot him during a rushed robbery. Who else would leave a Rolex? There were friends and family along with the one paragraph story on page eleven of the local paper but Bobby was forgotten. Stevie tried to figure out who had shot his friend, but after a few days he accepted it as a fact of life. Bobby was dead and the street lived on. Even glorified back alleys like Filbert Street.

It was late Saturday afternoon on Filbert Street and 63$^{rd}$ Street bristled with life. She was an old lady dressed in an overcoat. Her wig was stylishly gray, but solid as a rock. The cart she pushed in front of her seemed almost more for support than the convenience of carrying groceries. In her other arm she carried her purse. She stared to the ground more concerned for her next step than anything on the street walking toward her.

It was a kid, it was Pee Wee on Filbert Street. As soon as she turned the corner onto Filbert Street she became a target. Her pace was slow, steady and constant. What little he saw of old ladies he knew they kept big money in their purses and thus he figured this old lady was no different. He focused in on her purse. She couldn't have known what was coming. Even Pee Wee didn't see. It was so simple grab the purse and run. He was half way down the block while she had managed perhaps ten feet. He began to run, she plotted her next step. His last robbery, where he had shot Bobby, he managed to put over six hundred dollars into his pocket. This one would be better, this was a purse.

*Anonymous*

He ran by and grabbed the purse.

It would have been simple if she didn't hang on. Not only did she hang on but in short order she began swinging the cart hitting him on the side. He ducked as if a joke, she swung again.

"Come on lady give me your purse."

"help, help."

She was screaming but her body was too weak. She could only whimper. Across the street a curtain dropped, away from view.

"Lady give me the purse or I kill you."

He jumped up and down trying to emphasize his point.

She just swang that cart.

"Get away from me child. Get away you devil, you devil."

Each time she swang.

An old whiskered man laughed on a step next to what appeared to be a junk yard. It was a sight...

Pee Wee pulled out a gun and shot her.

He was aiming for the eye but he got her in the forehead, she was trying to duck.

The curtain raised and the old man stopped laughing.

Pee Wee had his money.

********

Muhammad missed his flight, much less the posters. The cops had questioned him a half a dozen ways from Sunday, and it was only Saturday.

"Who shot first?"

"Did you see the lookout"

"What kind of coat was he wearing?"

"Was he wearing a coat?"

"Why were you in town, Mr. Smith...Mr. Muhammad Smith."

"What posters?"

"You mean these posters?"

"Did the old guy have the gun on him or to the side somewhere?"

"You with this million man thing buddy?"

On and on; different cops, leading questions and bad coffee. His day was shot. He could stay until tomorrow but he wanted the comforts of home. Perhaps it was a wasted effort anyway, the Boy Scouts already had half the buses in Pittsburgh. Maybe he just wanted to take a trip. At 11:44 that night at the airport he threw the posters in the thrash. There were fifty in the bunch. Long after he was on his flight the airport janitor performed his rounds until he came across this one thrash can. In spite of his workman's clothes he wore a simple, plain box top hat. He was a Sunni Muslim. In Charlie's ignorance he had placed a Sunni Muslim in prominent view on his Million Man March poster. He was unaware of the deep separation that existed between the Black Sunni Muslims and the Black Nation of Islam Muslims. This janitor held himself in a certain dignity as many janitors do. He looked to the posters, the 'light', the unity, the brotherhood...

## BLACK MAN
## PILGRIMAGE OF FAITH
## THE MILLION MAN MARCH

*Anonymous*

By time Charlie got home all of the buses in Pittsburgh were sold out.

********

He hadn't checked his balance since Thursday night when it was about 50 grand. Sunday morning seemed like a good time to start things off. The phone, the digits, the balance...

"One Hundred, Twenty Seven Thousand, Four Hundred, Eighty Nine Dollars, And, Sixty Four, Cents." Hanging up the phone he still couldn't bring himself to smile. But with the thought of death still in his mind he dialed a number. It was the Franklin Answering Service.

"Good morning, This is Charles Smith. My account number is 495867...Yes. Thank you. I would like to change the price on that account from forty dollars to fifty for the Philly calls...Yes, that's correct. And that takes effect immediately correct?"

"Yes sir, I can put it on delay if you like."

"No, I want immediately. You know on second thought, for the calls from New York change it from forty to sixty.

"Ok. Will that be all today sir?"

"Yeah that's all. Thank you, thank you very much."

"Alright sir you have a nice day."

It was almost 11AM Sunday morning, the most segregated hour in America. It was a long time since Muhammad wore a dark suit to Church. And this one was brand new. Part of the splurge he allowed himself on Thursday along with the new shoes and the hundred-dollar purple necktie, against a rose colored shirt. He brought it on Walnut Street after seeing it in GQ magazine...He took them for their word: He was sharp. He got into his Cadillac and was on his way.

The Second Street AME church on Second Street was magnificent. A creation of 18$^{th}$ Century Negroes led by Richard Allen after the Methodist church suddenly on a Sunday morning at 11AM in 1756 restricted Richard and his friends to the balcony. Their reaction was immediate and they left the Church that very day to create the Second Street African Methodist Episcopal Church in 1756.

Muhammad was late, all the better. The usher showed him to a seat but he shook his head and pointed to the front. He walked past her with a smile and proceeded to the front. The choir rose at the directors signal and Muhammad found his way to the seat that he wanted. He caused a polite stir as he made his way through the row to the seat that he wanted.

His grandmother looked to the slight movement and was shocked to see Muhammad. The church began to sing. Once situated next to his grandmother he began to sing. She slapped him on the arm in loving welcome. He finally smiled. She marveled at his hair and his new suit. He just looked ahead reaching into his inside pocket. When the preacher said "Amen" he gave her the check.

*'One Hundred Ten Thousand..........DOLLARS'.*

Hand to cheek, she was surprised. Then he kissed her on the cheek. And the old broad cried. Halleluiah
"HALLELUIAH!!!"

*Anonymous*

She jumped to her feet in the middle of the song. Then with the inevitable embarrassment she sat back down. He hugged her, she hugged back.

After church there was lunch at the Bellevue Stratford. And then a stroll to Rittenhouse Square where, walking the streets of downtown cosmopolitan Philadelphia, he explained the success of his buses and the tragedy of Pittsburgh. Before they knew it they were at 20th and Walnut sitting in a park. Soon it was 4 o'clock. He grabbed a cab back to his car and drove his grandmother home.

"There was a old lady who got shot on 63$^{rd}$ Street. They say it was a child who killed her too, just like happened to you in Pittsburgh. Another boy about 14 years old."

"Humph, grandmom what's happening to Black people. I mean where does such anger come from in a fourteen year old kid?"

"Only the Lord knows Charlie."

There had to be more. There had to be.

Dropping his Grandmother off after yet another cup of coffee he went to pay off his next biggest bill… Stevie. Today it would be no problem to find Stevie. Stevie wanted to see him and had set up a meet at the Havana club for 5 o'clock. Stevie put a change on that and insisted they meet at B&B's at 15th and South. Mac wasn't too much on that Buppie/Yuppie stuff: A pretty picture, such lies. As always Stevie was late. Then there he was. He opens the door and walks in to the beat of "For the Love of Money" which played on the juke box. This seemed to fit well with his red suit atop a blue turtle neck adorned with a few bits of gold jewelry.

*The Adventures of Muhammad Smith and The Million Man March*

"CC and coke."

The bartender, Matt, jumped right to it. This was a man who deserved respect…the big tip kind.

"Yes sir."

"So you lookin' sharp. What up, you went to church?"

"Well as a matter of fact, yeah I went to church today. I guess you just said goodnight to Miss Black America."

"My brother, you would be guessing right."

"So why are we here today Stevie?"

"What, why is we here. Why is we here. Nigger do you got my money, I mean Nigger Please. You got's to help a brother."

With a sip and a smile Stevie was so cool.

"Far be it from me to keep a man from his hard earned money."

"How Miss Sally doin'?"

"She's alright I saw her today. You know the church thing."

"Man one of my ace boon's got kilt the other day."

"Where was this at?"

"They found him on Filbert just offa 63$^{rd}$ Street. And I had just talked to that nigger about an hour before he got shot."

"Ain't that where the old lady got shot yesterday?"

"Yeah man I been thinkin' the same thing."

"What's up with Black People Stevie, I mean are they monkeys or what? I don't get it. What's goin' wrong?"

"Black People, Black People, what you talkin' 'bout Black People. What about John Wayne Gacy and the Son o' Sam and half the trailer thrash in the country that claim they descended from Jessie James. Nigger puhleese. See, see you one of them 'flower from flower' niggers."

"Flower from flower, I don't get it."

Stevie sipped his CC and Coke.

"You think that flowers come from flowers. HA! Flowers come from dirt nigger and we the best dirt that America ever did see and ever will have."

"So you're saying that Blacks are dirt?"

"That gave birth to the American flower. Yeah I said it and don't got no problem wit it. If it won't for the so called Negro them Europeans would come over here and started Europe all over again."

"So you've given this some thought."

"I want mine like Kennedy got his. Shoot, he make a million dollars runnin' whiskey with Al Capone but they catch me with a joint and say they keepin' America pure. Nigger please, get a grip. You got my money, I gotta' go sell some dope."

# Free at Last: LOVE, AMERICAN STYLE

Charlie sipped his wine, still smiling. The bill was paid. Now it was Carmillias turn.

6:30PM was the routine meeting time and Stetsons was the place. Sometimes they would catch a movie first or maybe enjoy a walk down Walnut or South Street but the nightcap would always be a drink at Stetson's, her neighborhood bar. It was always Carmillia's call, her show. This was not a new thing but today Chuckie gave it thought. By mutual, unspoken agreement this was the extent of their world. No dinner with the family or meeting the parents, only Sunday night. Everything was cool as long as he kept his place.

She got there a little before seven. Her light coat was open revealing the tight short dress that clung to her body. Her hair was smartly cut to the bottom of her neck and with him in sight her body began to bounce, which gave a certain bounce to the low neckline of her dress. For a White girl she had real hips, which suddenly seemed to sway in his imagination. Once he imagined that they would marry and raise a family but tonight he only wanted one thing. At his bar stool she arrived leaning forward with a perfect view of her neckline and gave a kiss to his cheek.

"Hi pumpkin."

"Hey Carm."

"New suit, new hair….Mmmmm you didn't warn me. You look great."

When she sat her dress slid up her thighs and soon became the focus of his attention.

"So Carm you got any surprises for me?"

"Chuckie sex is always a surprise."

"Well since you put it that way let's have a surprise party tonight, I'll bring my friend Little Richard."

"And I'll bring little Betty Beaver."

"All we need now is a gift."

The drinks went quickly and they walked the short block to her apartment.

Her coat and his jacket were soon on the couch just after a short but embraceable kiss. Suddenly she was submissive but she took him by the hand and into her bedroom.

Pulling him to her she embraced for a long kiss with her arms holding him tight as her hands cradled his neck and then his head. Feeling the sweet welcome of her body he gently pushed her away to unbutton his shirt. She took the opportunity to lift her tight dress up and over her head and off of her body. There stood the delicacy of her body with only a shadow of underwear.

Through it all he could clearly see the joy he had come to know so well. She stepped back into his arms pushing off the shirt he had yet to unbutton but the single button fell to the floor as her hands then found their way to his zipper and all that separated him from her. Before his pants fell to the floor, she was on her knees so that she could enjoy all that he had to offer. Little Richard no longer was little.

Still this was no match for her voracious appetite. His legs quivering he stumbled into the bed where she was quick to follow, with a heat so intense her two remaining pieces of dress seemed to melt off of her skin. The drippings of her desire found their way atop of him where he instantly held tight.

The kissing seemed to ignite of it's own purpose.

Her purpose was to grab his body into a roll where he would be on top.

His purpose were the soft mounds of flesh he felt upon his chest, surely they would be like nectar to his mouth and tongue, but there was no ignoring the moist Betty Beaver which held the forbidden fruit.

A taste he could not forget.

Her hands rubbed his head as he devoured all that lay before him.

Now it was she who quivered at every touch.

Enjoying the taste of her skin

his destination was far more

than the belly button that he now caressed

with the intermittent probings of his now hot tongue.

With the softest touch she pulled him to her so that they were now

eye to eye,

kiss to kiss

and body to body.

The gift had finally arrived.

An hour later they lay beneath the sheets.

"Chuckie?"

*Anonymous*

"Yeah Carm."

"I love you."

He remained silent.

"Chuckie?"

"Yeah."

"Do you love me?"

He sat up in the bed.

"Carm does this mean that I can meet your parents say hi to your boss and take you on rides through the streets of North Philly?"

"Honey it doesn't have to be like that. We can have a life right here in Center City."

"Carm we both know that outside of these downtown wannabe rich bars and the confines of your bedroom this world ain't puttin' up with no Negro with a White woman even if it is 1995. And as far as love is concerned, this is just a good time Carm, nothing more than a weekly release for me and you."

"Chuckie I want you to live with me."

"Carm, I got other plans."

"…Did you meet one of those Black hussies?"

"Black 'hussies' hunh?"

"I didn't mean it like that Chuckie."

"Carm, don't you see that any 'love' we could ever hope to have would be full of 'I didn't mean it like that'?"

"Chuckie why is this so hard, I mean a million guys would love to have me and…"

"Not a million guys named Chuckie Carm."

"I thought this would make you happy. Forget it Chuckie, just forget it."

Chuckie sits with his arms resting on bent knees and stares into the darkness.

*The Adventures of Muhammad Smith and The Million Man March*

"Carm, I don't think I can make it next week…I got a special project on the 16th and I'm going to need the whole weekend to set it up."

Her head falls to his shoulder, full of apology.

"Baby, don't leave me."

"No it's not about tonight or leaving you. I have to go to the Million Man March."

"You mean that Black, OJ thing, no Chuckie not you. You're so…you're above that."

"It's not a OJ thing or a Black thing Carm. It's business."

"Isn't that a religious charity kinda thing?"

He smiles with insight.

"The Nation is known for many things Carm but charity ain't one of 'em."

"I'm sitting here Chuckie, pouring my heart out to you and you tell me you can't move in cause ya Black. Chuckie those days are over. We can live wherever we want."

"We can't live in North Philly."

"But Chuckie who wants to live in North Philly. The people who live in North Philly, don't even want to live in North Philly. Chuckie we're lovers, let's be friends."

Again silence.

"Look it ain't about you and me. It ain't about what we talkin' about. It's business Carm. Next week is about business."

"So do you love me?"

"Don't you want to know what the business is?"

"Do you love me?"

"No."

*Anonymous*

She stormed from the room into the bathroom. The echo has such an effect on crying. By time she returned, he was dressed.

"Look Carm, I'll see you on the next go round."

********

Monday morning couldn't come fast enough. Taking into account the money he had paid out yesterday, by Monday it had increased to about 75K. He was full of ideas. And it all turned on Stephanie. She had the numbers. She had contacts from here to LA. She knew people who did bus trips for a living to, of all places, Washington DC. Walking through her seventh floor office he was confident beyond his personality.

"Hello Miss Harris. And how are we today?"

"Not as good as you, that's obvious."

"Miss Harris you ain't seen nothin' yet."

"Well Stephanie ain't here right now but she said if'in you come to wait right here. She be right back."

"Where's she at?"

"In the bathroom. It's that time of month again."

"OK…Miss Harris…, I'll just sit right over here."

"Want me to go and get her."

"No that's OK, I'll just wait."

Sitting there by the front door he saw a fox of a female walk through. She stopped, looked behind her and along came the most He-man woman Charlie had seen in quite some time. They were together, practically hand in hand…tsk, tsk.

"Muhammad, I was expecting your call."

He looked to his right, down the hall

*The Adventures of Muhammad Smith and The Million Man March*

"Good morning Stephanie and how are you my African Daisy."

Smiling in disbelief she returns the compliment as best she could.

"Come on into my office Muhammad."

He enters her cramped jail cell sized office and moves the papers accordingly so that he can sit down. She looks at him, somewhat amazed.

"So what is it about these buses Muhammad and the Million Man March?"

"I saw Raheem last week. He says a lot of people want to go to the March. Is that true?"

"Yeah, we had a few stragglers but after the OJ thing, everyday more and more people want to go and they're calling us to find out how to go but we can't find any buses. No one in the city can find a bus. Do you got buses Muhammad? And what's all this talk about Boy Scouts in Pittsburgh?"

"In Philadelphia, I got a hundred buses, In Camden and Trenton I got twenty buses in each city. I got buses in New York, AC and Dover. And in Atlanta I got ten buses. Plus I can get a thousand more buses anywhere in the country if I want them."

"And just how did you get a thousand buses Muhammad?"

"I saw it coming Stephanie, right there at the burger joint, the difference between the Blacks and the Whites, the Rodney King thing and even little Miss Susan Smith. I saw it coming like a brick through the window."

"And now you got buses?"

From his inside jacket pocket he pulls out several folded papers and hands them to her.

*Anonymous*

"These are half of the contracts I have. I got the buses Stephanie."

"Why contracts, why not receipts?"

His excitement spilled over into a smile.

"Stephanie, it's so clear. When these White people realize that a million Negro men are really going to be in one place at one time, they're going to lock down everything in sight, including their buses."

"There you go with that 'Negro' word again. Things never change do they Muhammad…So now you want me to 'baby sit' some Boy Scouts?"

"…Listen Steph, I got buses in all of these places but really I'm at the mercy of the bus companies to act right. Really I need someone, anyone who I can trust in each city. Plus I really want to go to LA, Chicago, Dallas and everywhere else you can think of but I don't got the people. You do."

Just then Miss Harris came to the door.

"It's the NOW people on line two, they want to know somethin' about the Million Man March."

For a moment Stephanie and Muhammad just looked at each other.

"OK, thank you Miss Harris."

Then she turned back to Muhammad.

"Give me a second Mac, then we'll go get coffee."

No one had called him Mac except his closest of family, which of course, Stephanie once was.

At the 50 cent café they sat for a cup.

"So you want to use my connections for your buses…"

He nodded

"…What's in it for you?"

*The Adventures of Muhammad Smith and The Million Man March*

"Money."

"You have a surprising directness about you Muhammad."

"Is that a compliment?"

"…No just a dream."

"Sorry Steph, I don't got too much time for dreams right now. This thing is exactly one week away. So you're either with me or not. I know you need the buses."

She smiles with an intensity.

"I want ten dollars for every seat I fill. That means every city I organize."

"OK, done. So you have a taste for the dollar too."

"No. Make out all money to the organization, ISIS."

She extends her hand.

"So do we have a deal Mr. Muhammad Charles Smith?"

"Deal."

Almost like that he had thousands of customers. If the Peters/Mercury thing was true then he was set. No time for surprises though, he had to know now. He went to see Walter Peters one last time.

\*\*\*\*\*\*\*\*

"Yes miss, my name is Muhammad Charles Smith and I'm here to see Mr. Peters."

"Have a seat sir I'll tell him that you're here."

Muhammad took his seat in the plush office furniture scanning the corporate pictures that covered the walls of buses in far off locales. It was his, all his.

*Anonymous*

"Mr. Smith, no more Jerry curl. I'm impressed. Please come back to my office."

They sat in their respective seats.

"So have you come to do business or are you here to call me a flaming racist."

"You half Black ain't you?"

"Ahh, give that man a cigar. Then I can assume you want to do business."

"Can I get 10 buses in Chicago for this weekend?"

"If you have the $400, for each bus for each day you've got the best deal in the country. The company has jacked the price up to eight hundred for that day and there's even talk that they won't rent buses at all for the 16th, not for Washington. But then you have a contract, don't you Mr. Smith?"

"Yeah I got a contract. How bout that…What's in it for you Mr. Peters?"

"…Humph, what's in it for me…I suppose everybody hopes to get different things from this Million Man March Mr. Smith. I mean you want money, CNN wants a story and OJ, who we owe it all to, only wants a White woman. What do I want? What's it to you?"

"That comment, just before I left last time."

"I'm sorry Mr. Smith but you'll have to refresh my memory"

"The measure on the yardstick of silky hair."

"Ah yes, my mother told my father that a million times, but he never got it…"

Muhammad looked up at the picture on the wall.

"…As long as you measure yourself on the yardstick of silky hair, you'll never measure up."

"What does that mean?"

"Are you aware of the original sin Mr. Smith, most people, as a matter of fact, nobody knows it. Genesis two…"

"Seventeen. The tree of knowledge…"

"Of good…"

"And evil"

"I knew I was going to like you Mr. Smith."

"So what do that got to do with the Million Man March?"

"…How long do you think it would have taken an African to invent the light bulb Mr. Smith if the White man had never drew little red lines on your precious African map. How long would it of taken? Edison did it in 1879. Perhaps Africa would of stumbled across it in 1950, 1990 maybe even ten years from now in two thousand and five. Maybe never."

"You say some pretty insultin' stuff Mr. Peters."

"Oh you want a nice gentle truth Mr. Smith, a truth where you are EQUAL to the White Man."

"No, forget it. I'll just pay for the buses and le..."

"An African would have never invented the light bulb Mr. Smith…"

Muhammad rose to leave.

"They were getting along just fine with the sun…"

This caught Muhammad's attention.

"What's wrong with that Mr. Smith?"

"So that's why you want a million Black guys to go to Washington, for a light bulb?"

"Mr. Smith it was only in March that the naturally smart Japanese released nerve gas in their subways. It was only seventy years ago that the European invented it. And of the European, their concept of nationhood came crashing into the ground on April 6th of last year in Rawanda. By April 7th Mr. Smith, the African concept of tribal pride murdered one million people with one swipe of the machete. Tell me Muhammad, just what do you want to be equal to."

"You know mister for somebody who's half White you got a funny way of talking."

"It's the complete wrong direction Mr. Smith. You call this number and wire the money to this account whenever you need buses. Take them to Washington DC Mr. Smith. Lets see what the esteemed Mister Farrakhan has to say."

********

The day was still young. Perhaps an afternoon movie or a surprise trip to the Art Museum with Grandmom. Perhaps it was time to make a call to the account. He hadn't checked for a while. At a public phone on Broad Street, just south of City Hall he called the bank, the automated answer and then his digits. Despite all of his accurate predictions he was still surprised…

"Two Hundred Fifty Nine Thousand Eight Hundred Sixty Nine Dollars And Sixty Four Cents."

So now he had money, another roll of the dice. The only time he had ever come close was when he got his stock package after he was fired for smoking weed from the phone company. He brought IBM in '94 but sold it a few months later for Nextel…He thought he knew phones.

So what now for '95! A spending spree down Walnut Street, the most expensive street in the city. A donation to the Red Cross…Good for taxes, don't you know, or perhaps tracking down a White boy for some good weed. After all he hadn't had one good smoke since this thing started. For some idiotic reason he went to check on his mailing service. He wanted to be sure that was running smooth and that they were getting everything they needed from the answering service. A few calls to some of his bus operators. He could sense that Whites were starting to get squeamish over a million Negro men in one place at the same time, some of the bus operators may want to quit. It might be a good time to remind them of the definition of a contract. These things were done in good time, on a busy day where he had a lot of energy and money. Still at the end he could not escape the fact that he was alone.

# Muhammad Charles Smith: THIS IS YOUR LIFE

He was born Muhammad Charles Smith on December 9$^{th}$ 1956, the very day that the Montgomery boycott, started by one Rosa Parks, ended in complete victory. That Rosa had since been mugged by a Black guy, led some to say that the point was lost. But Muhammad never really cared one way or the other. He grew up with memories of the Three Stooges on the Sally Star show after school and the Gene London show with Walt Disney before school. Mass media had arrived. Thus for the young Charlie "yunk, yunk, yunk" took on a special meaning. For years all his mind really absorbed was the ABC's of CBS and NBC. His twin brother didn't get the TV thing, he was always outside. Yet from an early age his mother enjoyed the company of the quiet Muhammad and the TV.

He had seen things in his mother, like her wig, things he really didn't like. Like the times that she would shoot horse right next to him, the men who so often came and went: There were things he didn't like. But she was his protector, always siding with him in disputes with his brother or anyone else. It was a true display of the inherent love between mother and child. Then to see her for the last time in the funny farm, lost to the bureaucratic idiocy of public health. He never did get the full story of why his mother had killed Jay Livingston but the older he got the more he figured it out. Living with his grandmother was a mild transition, though she didn't like Gene London and Walt Disney. In fact she didn't like Disney at all, she said it was the Whitest thing in America.

Abraham, his brother, had learned sex as a toy, when he was six or seven. Muhammad didn't learn sex until sixteen or seventeen, when it became a frustration. Never the less the first of his joys was solitude. So he never really noticed that one of the four black girls in his elementary school was named Stephanie Morgan. Even then he only wanted to know White culture and the special school that his teacher and grandmother got him into was full of it. The Beatles, Herman's Hermits and right on up to Barry Manilow, it was clear even to his young eyes that Herman's Hermits had a future. The few times he had listened to James Brown all he heard were screams. He had no idea what it was about, this music that made his brother dance so well. In fact back then Muhammad saw nothing of value in Black, American, Negro culture. What did they invent, of any real significance, what was their global contribution... Africa? At this early age he had a clear understanding that he could never tell anyone that he was ashamed to be Black, colored, Negro, or whatever pretty name they gave. He was ashamed to be a nigger. A lifetime memory was him rushing out of the tub at seven years old thinking that if he combed his hair when it was wet it would retain it's silky (yet wet) quality. When he discovered that his great grandfather may have been White, he was overcome with pride. It was only the happenstance chance of hearing a rare, rare sermon on the original transgression of man against god, that Muhammad had changed his whole view. And he finally understood what James Brown was talking about.

He had only begun talking to Stephanie on a dare from his brother, but through the years she was getting persistent. Their relationship grew to a point where they enjoyed talking about class work and would manage a trip to a museum or a downtown movie. Still his 1971 TV trained mind had no concept of what to do next. Like Wally of "Leave it to Beaver" he had no idea how to get from one end of the couch to the other AND get your arm around the girl. In the mass media of 1971, sex did not exist, thus Muhammad was literally lost without a clue. It was Stephanie's persistence that had saved this virgin and introduced him to a real world. From time to time he was grateful for this.

His ten years in the Army went by quick, he barely realized he had acquired a skill until he met a phone guy who was in the Army. Another ten years flew by and now here he was on this night at Broad and Chestnut with two hundred grand in his pocket and not a clue of what to do. The city swirled.

\*\*\*\*\*\*\*\*

Only for kicks did Pee Wee come to the isolated basement classroom of his local school on this Monday morning. Most days, lately, he had been going downtown eating at McDonalds and buying fifty dollar sneakers. But today he came to school for fun, with his gun. Already in his 3rd grade class he was the bully, being the oldest and biggest had little to do with it, so no need to prove anything to the other kids. Mrs. Morris was another story.

"Takes your seats children. We've been over this before."

The children ran about as all children do around the world. Soon enough they were in their seats.

"Peter that is not your seat. Will you please get up and go to the back of the classroom."

"Mrs. Morris my name ain't Peter. It's Pee Wee."

"Alright, that's enough, will you please go to your seat Mr. Pee Wee?"

"Let me think about it. I want to make an educated choice."

"Fine, stay right there. Tell me Peter, you've been out of school for three days now. You wouldn't happen to have a note from your mother or anything, would you?"

Feigning confusion Pee Wee looks through his pockets.

"A note from mom, I know I got it."

"Peter, that's ok. Class open your math books to page twenty three."

She rises to the blackboard to begin the lesson.

"I got it. A note from my daddy."

"Peter when are you…"

She turned to face him

"going to grow…"

She didn't notice that it was big and shiny. She only noticed that it was a gun in the hands of a smiling illiterate child.

"So…who your daddy now Mrs. Morris?"

The class went silent.

"Pee Wee…"

Suddenly she knew his name.

"…put that down."

"Is my note good enough Mrs. Morris?"

"It's just fine Pee Wee. Put the gun down."

He began to sit, then just before he touched the wooden seat he stood back up.

"But Mrs. Morris…"

"Yes."

"Who your daddy?"

She stared him in the eye for as long as she could. He looked back with the gun easily to his side.

"You are. You are my daddy."

"Oh, Ok."

He took the seat at the front of the class. Calmly she spoke to the stunned class.

"Class read your books, I'm going to get a drink of water"

She made it to the end of the alphabet line when he stopped her.

"No."

She froze in her tracks

"You can't have no water."

Her only response was to listen for more instructions. After all he had the gun.

"I want you to take your seat. In the back of the class."

To emphasize his point he pointed the gun. She turned, towards the back and walked, near him, by him and then she went for the gun. A quick grab with both hands she missed, but got his wrist. This was

*The Adventures of Muhammad Smith and The Million Man March*

good because she now controlled his arm, but it was bad because he could still bend his hand and that's where the gun was. Meanwhile at the same time she was trying to hide behind his body, creating a certain circular momentum where they swung the gun around the room twice in a circle. The class was out of their mind. As the gun would point in their respective directions they would jump, run, holla, drop, duck or, in one case, just sit there and cry. Pee Wee saw an escape between her legs so he dropped to his knees and crawled between her braced but open legs. She followed bending forward as far as she could go, trying to pull the gun away from him. Her feet spread wider apart and her skirt slid up her thighs. Soon she was low enough that her head touched the floor with a little thump thus making a triangle with her two feet and almost leaving her stuck as she struggled to control the gun, now smack dab in the middle of her legs. Pee Wee stood up behind her jamming the gun between her awkward and triangulating body. By sliding her hair on the floor she was almost through her own legs when he gave a sudden jerk and broke free. First she rolled left and he shot left, then she rolled right and he shot to the right. And even though she slipped she made it to her feet amidst two more shots and ran for the door but he shot the door so she ran in the opposite direction, but in the corner a bullet ricocheted through the air. Then she turned for a quick dash to her desk and ducked under that but he shot at that too so she ran for the door, again, and almost made it but got shot dead. Just like that she dropped. Pee Wee was getting good at this.

For a brief second he walked up to admire his work. Turning to the stunned class he spoke, quickly.

"Yes! Yes, I'm bad. I'm the teacher."

The students could not articulate a response so they just looked at him. He looked back and spoke.

"Alright class dismissed."

They didn't move an inch.

"Well I don't know 'bout y'all but I'm leavin'. "

********

By time Muhammad got home it was all over the radio, on WHAT AM: Colin Powell would not be coming to the Million Man March. Apparently Farrakhan was on the David Brinkley Show yesterday and he extended an offer to OJ and Powell. Phone calls seeking comment from Powell were not returned. As far as OJ, well that was quickly forgotten. Even if, in all likelihood, it was OJ's life and not Farrakhan's words that would bring a million people into Washington DC.

Muhammad thought for a bit of the irony that two first generation Negro natives like Powell and Farrakhan from the Caribbean were so successful in America yet many American Blacks who could trace their lineage back into the South of the 1800's were stuck in the squalor of the inner city. There's something about the first generation of immigrants who came to America since 1776 he often thought. They got something that Indians and African-Americans, in that order, did not get and it can never be got. Soon enough even Colin Powell felt the pull of the extreme grass root appeal of this march and issued a statement read by an assistant, Peggy Cifrino, who said "Mr. Powell was out of town with commitments and can not attend the march but

*The Adventures of Muhammad Smith and The Million Man March*

that he does support it's purpose". When the female announcer got over the 'Peggy' part she started to talk about OJ's response and right away laughter.

"And the Negro cannot be found...Well moving right along back to Mr. Colin Powell"

"...Imagine that Brother OJ with the Cifrino girls."

The DJ spoke with contempt

"Never in this lifetime sister"

The sidekick kicked in but Muhammad wasn't amused. He turned back to his familiar TV and heard the proper news.

"Third grader kills teacher...Details at eleven."

He looked at the news promo and thought for a brief intense second of his recent experience in Pittsburgh. Then he turned away from local realities and turned the channel to CNN for national affairs. There was only one story he wanted to hear. With each passing day there was more and more news from the proper news about the Million Man March. Would there really be a million people, a million Black men? What do they want? It would take mass media and the mass public another couple of days to understand the organizers of this 'march'. In spite of this coming event OJ was still in the news. About a week after his release America wanted to know his every move. NBC had planned an interview with him for the following night. The audience would be humongous but the protests were deafening. How did he get away? What could be done so this would never happen again? Change the constitution...make juries illegal? Could justice still be served with a civil suit for wrongful death? It just didn't stop. And even though CNN would give only polite mention of the Million Man March, Muhammad knew that with each claim of a perfect justice system, more and more people, Black people, would want to go to the march. Richard Pryor had taught Black America a thing or two about justice (just us).

Oh but so what, what did it matter why a bunch of people were going to Washington? Charlie took pride in the fact that he saw it comin' and capitalized. No matter what anyone's definition of "Black Power" was, he was gonna' have some green. Tomorrow, first thing, he had to see Stephanie. It was clear that her connections and organization were key to any expansion. Perhaps it was a good time to give Abraham a call in jail.

Abraham Charles and Muhammad Charles Smith were born the children of sixteen year old Mary Louise Smith, father unknown. After a family tragedy, at the age of twelve, they moved in with their grandmother Sally Mae Smith. By this time Abraham and Muhammad had set their separate paths. Abe was of the street, the party, the excitement. Muhammad was the homebody looking for solitude and silence. Abe had abandoned school by the 10th grade. But Muhammad found a comfort not in the achievement of A's but the respect of his teachers. They always said he was smart. So for his entire school life he only did just enough to hear the praise of potential. For outside of the school walls there was a different world and knowing the difference between the American and Russian Revolutions meant absolutely nothing. There were no theories of perfection to fight for in this neighborhood. It was this potential and his Grandmother's plotting that allowed him to be chosen for a pilot program that bused him

*The Adventures of Muhammad Smith and The Million Man March*

to the finest schools in the city. This inherently meant that they were white schools. Not like working class Kensington white but upper class Chestnut Hill white. He was ten when he arrived at the John Story School on the northern end of Germantown Avenue. This is where he meant Stephanie but they never talked. In fact at John Story Jenks Elementary, Charlie didn't talk to Black people much at all. His world, by choice was White. It was 1966 and the whole concept of "Black is Beautiful" was new and there was still many a man wearing a process in their hair and ladies buying the latest brand of skin lightening cream. Muhammad admired the White world full of superheroes, gods and legends. Blacks had none of this in 1966. In 1966, even John Henry was a stranger to most Blacks. Even as John Henry's basic theme was man against machine, Black America flocked to the machine that the White man had built. The White man was in charge and Charlie wanted to be White.

He finally spoke to Stephanie in the 9th grade, in spite of her radical Black beliefs. He only did it on a dare from his brother. Soon though Muhammad and Stephanie found a common joy in their education. And even at the age of the 9th grade when all they could imagine to do was go to a museum or maybe an educational movie, there was an attraction.

Once she got pregnant everything changed. She stayed in school and got the proper rest. He enrolled in an after school program that would land him an automatic job with the city. When the baby came he was surprised that the infant was so dark and didn't look anything like him. After the blood test his depression led him into the Army for ten years through

*Anonymous*

Kansas, Korea and Arizona. He continued smoking weed in the Army with White girls who wanted to smoke him. Coming back home in 1983 anything close to a childhood friend was either dead, at work or forgotten. He enrolled into a two year College for the next seven years but lucked out with a job at MCI where he managed to land a decent wage. In one of his classes he met Carmillia and they started a sex affair. In spite of losing his job in 1993 she stayed with him, every Sunday night. But now even she was gone. This thought of being alone was starting to nag him. At least he and Abraham held a strong respect for each other. He would have to call the state pen about an hour ahead of time to arrange the call. But it was his brother and he had something to say. But first he had to co-ordinate the final push.

The next day began with the morning routine of a toilet stoop, clean shave and a hot shower. Abandoning his usual blazer and jeans, he dressed in his $500.00 sweater from Boyd's along with matching pants and the alligator shoes.

"Good Morning Miss. Harris."

"Well ain't we lookin' spiffy."

"Thank you Miss Harris. Stephanie is here isn't she?"

"Yeah she's in her office talkin' to the National Council of Negro Women. Go on take yourself a seat, she'll be out in a second. Boy she was looking for you yesterday."

"Why would I hold such an honor?"

"Said everyone wants to go to the March and somethin' 'bout you had some buses."

"Humph, imagine that."

"Ain't that somethin' about that 3$^{rd}$ grade child?"

"I really haven't been following the news that much. What happened?"

"Lawd this little boy done killed his teacher and now don't nobody know where he live, and now they talking they don't even know his real name."

"Progress hunh?"

"Lawd, lawd."

"MUHAMMAD is that you?"

Stephanie called from her office. He got up and walked in.

"Hello Stephanie."

"Take a seat." She was still on the phone with The Council. "Hey I agree but we still need to include our message…I spoke to Tommy too, he said the Senator wasn't interested…Listen Eva, I got to go. I gotta jump on this march thing…It's like out of the woodwork girl, now everybody wants to go…Yeah I heard Jessie was changing his tune too. The Million Man March, we'll see…Ok, goodbye."

She gave him a smile of relief

"Whew. I thought I'd never get off that phone"

"And good morning to you Stephanie."

"Ahh Muhammad, stop being so melodramatic. It doesn't suit you. We got work to do. Everyone wants a bus."

"Where at?"

"Everywhere: Tuskegee, Howard, Dallas, Lincoln. Everywhere but bus owners won't rent. They say it's too dangerous, their insurance won't cover it."

"That's a lie."

"I know, but they own the bus."

*Anonymous*

"I got a thousand buses and maybe more and I can have them in any city with twenty four hour notice."

"Are you sure because we had a few folks come in with canceled rentals."

"I got contracts Stephanie. I saw this coming from a mile away."

"Muhammad the way this thing is going a thousand buses will not be enough. Everyday it's more and more people who want to go. Even some of the big guys Mfume, Jackson, who were ignoring it a week ago are trying to get in on it now."

"Mfume might go. I thought the NAACP was definitely out."

"Maybe that's what they say in public but I think Mfume is going to go."

"That reminds me that I don't have any buses in Baltimore."

"Twenty four hour notice right?" She asked.

"If we're going to set up these buses, we have to start now. Do you have a list of cities?"

"Well I want to make a few more calls, but easily by this afternoon."

"Good I want to call Abraham today, which usually takes time so I can meet you back here this afternoon."

"Listen you can grab that back office back there and make all the calls you want. I know you want to talk about money and I want to do that today."

"Ok, thank you"

Then she spoke matter of factly.

"Look we're going to knock this week out and put it behind us…Alright?"

*The Adventures of Muhammad Smith and The Million Man March*

Muhammad didn't know if she was apologizing or planning.

"Ok Stephanie, anything you say."

********

"Hey Mac, what's up?"

"What's up bro?"

"Well Mac in prison the ceiling is only 7 feet high. So prison ain't up Mac."

"Yeah I guess you got a point there Abe."

"How's Grandmom? Is James treating you right?"

"Grandmom's fine, I have it on good authority. And James, well he's just James but it don't matter. I don't work for him anymore."

"You got fired from McDonalds?"

"It's not McDonalds, it's Fast Food Delite."

"Yeah, yeah whatever. You got fired?"

"No I quit."

"What made you do that?"

"I got two hundred grand in the bank Abe."

At first glance Abe knew his brother wasn't lying or joking. After this realization he got a twinkle in his eye.

"Atlantic City?"

"No."

"The number, you hit that fantasy five thing?"

"The Million Man March."

"You mean that Muslim thing?"

"Yep."

"You ain't no Muslim; Sunni or Nation."

"Buses."

Abe got quiet and thought for a second.

"Buses, you rentin' out buses to the march."
"You got it."
"So what you gonna do with all that money bro?"
"I don't know, how much does a good lawyer cost?"
"You mean the OJ kind or the Alabama kind?"
"Let's try for the Philly kind."
"That sounds right nice. You still smoking the good stuff?"
"Not lately."
"Grandmom still on your stuff?"
"I moved from there years ago. Why do you always say that?"
"You still messin' wit' that white girl?"
"I saw her Sunday as a matter of fact."
"Yeah that's right y'all always had that Sunday thing goin' on."
"But not this coming up Sunday. I got too much to do with this march stuff."
"Hey bro?"
"Yeah man."
"Where they marchin' to?"
"I don't think anyone knows Abe."
"Imagine that."
"Imagine that."
"You seen mom yet, heard anything about her? I mean is she alive, is she dead?"
"I haven't seen her since the funny farm, just like you."
"I miss her Mac."
"So did you get any good behavior, did they change your release date?"
"Nope, still September the 11$^{th}$, 2001"

"Well, we'll have a party on that day."
"See you later man."
"Bye."

First order of business after the march: Get Abe a OJ lawyer.

## From Philly to Bel-Air: THE FRESH PRINCE

The afternoon was tight. Stephanie had the list of cities that were asking for buses. As far west as LA to north of Boston and on over to South Beach of Miami. There were phone calls to determine how many people were going, how many buses were needed. They drew out a schedule of prices. Anything west of Pittsburgh and south of Columbia, South Carolina was Eighty dollars. Stephanie would get her ten bucks a head. If it was Chicago and beyond the price was $135, plus two day trips would have to be considered. Denver and Vegas would have to pay $185 and a two day trip was a fact. When Muhammad saw LA on Stephanie's list he insisted that the price would have to be at least $200 and the reality that it would take three days to drive from LA was part of the package. They would have to leave on Friday and no later than Saturday 12 noon. That would be long trip but there was a rumor that Jim Brown, while not going himself (maybe it was a Malcolm thing), was quietly organizing buses to make the trip. Everything that Peters had said about Mercury Bus Incorporated turned out to be solid. The

*The Adventures of Muhammad Smith and The Million Man March*

phone number that Peters had given him was answered by a female dispatcher who gave him a confirmation number and the promise that the buses would be waiting at the bus station of a particular city. Usually though Stephanie arranged for the buses to meet at locations picked by her associates in any given city. Some places like Cheyenne, Wyoming only needed one bus. Then there were others that were surprising like Tulsa, Oklahoma which also had a surprising history. They were asking for ten buses right off the bat and before it was over they had twenty and still wanted more. Oklahoma, Stephanie said, had a large Black population. A reflection of Blacks running west back in slavery days and the Army back then thought they were suited to deal with the Indians. By the end of the day they had almost half of the stated thousand buses rented out. Not in piecemeal one ticket increments but whole cities at once. So really, the thought would hit him later that he had made, maybe, one and a half million dollars. The money, by mutual agreement with Stephanie, would transfer the next day. Stephanie said the best made plans with the most steadfast of friends often fell apart at the last minute over money. She was helpful and sometimes shrewd. Like when speaking to C.H.I.P., the 'Cleveland Homeless In Progress'.

"See Sam that's what I mean. Last time we gave you a break with Detroit. I mean Sam it's like you don't never want to pay. You got money. After all it was you who asked me for a bus....Well, that's all well and good but the truth of the matter is that I'm sure that there are a dozen churches in Cleveland looking for a bus.... Fine. Have a good trip brother. Bye."

"Was that one of your 'steadfast friends'?"

"Oh Sam, Sam alright. I have to deal with him two or three times a year."

"What was his beef?"

"He wanted to go for free. That ain't happenin' today. This is too important."

"So you feeling this Million Man thing hunh?"

"Muhammad, something is missing. Something ain't right. Young kids killing each other."

"That's common in congested areas. London in the 1890's, New York in the 1900's with the Five Points Gang. You taught me that Stephanie. You just mad cause you livin' in it"

"But still with Blacks there is no cohesion, no common goal. George Bush dares to hold up Clarence Thomas as the epitome of what we should be. Something's missing Muhammad and I think Farrakhan can put it right. With a wave of that man's hand a lot of this nonsense would stop."

"Yeah I heard him speak, but I wonder…"

The PA system.

"Miss Morgan. You have Cleveland on line two."

"…That's right Sam Eighty dollars…The deal ain't set until the money is in the account."

She smiled over the phone.

"…You know this thing is snowballin'. Don't be late Sam. Ok…bye…take care."

She hung up the phone and turned to her one time friend.

"Let's do lunch."


It was a cute Chinese restaurant at 16$^{th}$ and Chestnut with booths and even a seat in the rear. Charlie ordered

*The Adventures of Muhammad Smith and The Million Man March*

Beef and Broccoli, his regular. Stephanie got General Tso's Chicken with hot sauce

"So Muhammad what have you been doing with yourself since 12$^{th}$ grade?"

"It's been that long?"

"You went off to the army and I never heard from you again."

"Yeah I guess it was kinda sudden hunh?"

"Kinda? How is Abe doing? I heard he was in jail, in Alabama?"

"Yep, Alabama. He got caught runnin' some weed from Louisiana."

"You still smoke that stuff Muhammad?"

"It's been a while."

"You still smoke...How's Miss Sally doing?"

"She's fine, and Raheem?"

"He started pre-med last month."

"I heard. You did good with him Stephanie..."

They looked slightly away from each other. Then she looked back to him...

"I managed. No biggie...So tell me Muhammad what on Earth made you reserve a thousand buses a month ago, when almost nobody even heard of the Million Man March?"

"It was the White crowd at the fast food joint. They so hated OJ. And then the Black employees were so sympathetic. There was a energy there, a synergy. And then it hit me about Rodney King and even that Susan Smith lady."

"The one who drowned her kids."

"Yeah that's right. And then believe it or not I was looking at Jackie Gleason come up with a buses in Harlem gimmick and it just hit me."

*Anonymous*

"Jackie Gleason hunh?"

"Jackie Gleason."

"You still go with that White girl?"

The waiter brought their food.

"What White girl?"

"Don't get Black on me Muhammad, I've known your Oreo butt since 6th grade. Donna Perry told me she's seen you a lot at Stetson's with some White girl. Do you remember Donna Perry?"

"No I can't say that rings any particular bells."

"She was the Black girl who was in 5th grade at Jenks. She had a crush on you. We all did but you were always with the Whites."

"Who was that lady on the phone with your underwear?"

She smiled

"That was Joanne, she's just a friend."

"One of those early morning Saturday friends. The good kind."

"You had a cousin, James right?"

"Yeah he owns the fast food joint I was working at."

"You were working in a take out joint. I always thought you would be a lawyer or an engineer."

"Where did that come from?"

"You were so good with the Whites, I figured you for the perfect token."

"You're not going to believe this but I had one habit that didn't fit well with corporate America. I laughed too loud."

"Laughed too loud?"

"My boss told me I was too happy and gave me a piss test."

"For the man who hasn't smoked in a while."

"...I saw your mom. I was sorry to hear about your dad."

"It was a few years ago, heart attack. He always liked you Muhammad."

"I know."

By the end of the day they had the chaperones for Pittsburgh and had ordered ten buses for Montreal. This had grown beyond a count of dollars and buses. This was no longer a snowball, it had become a steaming locomotive. In a certain reality by Tuesday night everybody who was going had made their plans. Muhammad's ears perked when he heard two young women outside of Stephanie's office challenging each other on their belief in the Million Man March...almost challenging each other as to how Black they were.

"Girl you don't even believe in the Million Man March."

"What is Farrakhan gonna do? Say the White man is white. You can't say that stuff in public."

"Why not, they say that Rodney King is a buffoon in public."

"Rodney King IS a buffoon."

"See that's what I mean."

\*\*\*\*\*\*\*\*

All in all it was a nice day with Stephanie. Her expertise at taking trips to Harrisburg and Washington was invaluable. Her contacts with other social groups across the nation were priceless. He left her office a little after five and went for dinner, alone, at the Down

Town restaurant on 20th Street. He liked the baked fish with old time mashed potatoes and vegetables and on weekdays they gave a free glass of wine. He never shared names with the waitresses even though he had seen them for years. He enjoyed the solitude as much as the fish. Then from a glance of his eye he saw Stephanie walking outside on Chestnut Street. He ran to the door.

"STEPHANIE."

She turned from her jaunt to 30th Street Station and saw Muhammad. They had a nice dinner. And later they even made it to Havana's on South Street and danced a dance or two. When he finally drove her home they shared a few laughs about school days, and other current events. They spoke of everything except Raheem. Maybe they would of come around to that but now sitting in a car in front of Stephanie's house drew the attention of Joanne who opened the door and looked.

"Who is that, the friend?"

"Yeah that's Joanne. She loves me so, God bless her heart."

"Look I'll probably see you tomorrow."

"Ok."

He got home just in time for the 11 o'clock news.

"And now here's Vernon Odom."

"Yes Jim. It appears the school board has been caught with their pants down. It was only yesterday that an often absent young student decided to come to school and wreck havoc into the life of 23 year old Jennifer Myers who was shot and killed by the a 3rd grade student known only as 'Pee Wee'. It appears the student's last name, address and even age are a complete mystery to the school board and the police. Captain John Kulinski of the Philadelphia Police Homicide unit.

"Yeah Vernon it seems that the child's identification hasn't been updated since 1989. We're looking into the possibility that his name was changed from Jihad Ak MaDeea and that he no longer lives at the 5$^{th}$ Street Motel, apartment C45 as stated in 1989."

"Do you have a picture?"

"It seems the child's family never ordered any class pictures so at this time the department has not secured a likeness of the individual except to say that he's ten years old."

"So Jim there you have it. Be on the look out for a ten year old child armed and extremely dangerous. Live at the Round House, I'm Vernon Odom."

That story got little more than a minute Charlie noticed. He turned to CNN, Farrakhan and the march was starting to get ten or fifteen minutes out of the hour. An event that wasn't even on the horizon a week ago was slowly taking center stage. At the core of these CNN reports was the question "What are a million Black men going to do in Washington?" This thought was laced with the suspicion that there would be violence. They had yet to understand the organizers of the Million Man March: The Nation of Islam. Anyone with any understanding of Black urban culture knew that the Nation was not about riots or any other street crime. In fact just the opposite, this collection of men in suits and bow ties with their woman covered in flowing sheets from head to toe were always a symbol of order. To those with no understanding of this urban culture the Black Muslims represented a menacing collection of tough looking Black men hiding behind a facade of suit and tie. If Farrakhan played his cards right all Black men would wear the suit and tie. But CNN hadn't focused on Farrakhan yet. They were wondering if a million Black men were going to show up. All they had to do was ask Charlie.

********

It was 12 midnight and Stevie was at the ChopShop Bar and Grill on Fairmont next to Becky's, a Black fish joint near 22$^{nd}$ Street. He was here with Larry a white guy he knew from a check-cashing joint near 52$^{nd}$ Street. Larry owned the Bar and Grill too. They were setting up a dope deal. There were a lot of White kids moving just south of Fairmont. It was almost becoming a ritzy neighborhood. Just north of Fairmont was the North Philly Ghetto. Larry and Stevie figured out that with a good supply these White boys could stop risking their lives in North Philly and buy their drugs in a safe environment. What Stevie didn't figure was that Larry had just got busted for Meth and Stevie was his ticket out of jail. Stevie was being set up big time. Larry claimed that he wanted a big first buy so that he could establish himself as the man with the good stuff. White boys always brought in bulk was the way Stevie saw it. Besides a ten kilo sale would be a right nice profit. This is what Stevie was thinking when Larry offered a hundred grand for the whole shebang. What he didn't see were the two FBI men, almost in stereotypical sunglasses, in the corner. They laughed, drank and agreed on a date next Tuesday. After all

*The Adventures of Muhammad Smith and The Million Man March*

Stevie would need a bit of time to set things up with the Puerto Rican boys from New York. They met today so that Larry could front him ten grand on the deal. When that money changed hands, Stevie was a goner. Oh the boom wouldn't come until next Tuesday but Stevie was busted all the same.

Pee Wee was home in his usual room. But now with a new TV just out of the box off to the side. His mother was Lord knows where but through a common quirk in the bureaucracy known as the school board, there was no real identification for this child who had killed a teacher. The police didn't have a picture. The only picture that Pee Wee knew of was on top of a milk crate in his mother's room. He brought her a TV too and for the last few days had even been buying her chicken wings from the Chinese store: One of his favorites.

It was the Fresh Prince Show. A cute tale of a Philly boy made good. There was just enough room for Pee Wee to imagine himself there in Hollywood, telling that Carl guy that he was stupid. Anyone could tell Carl was stupid. After a good laugh and a commercial, Pee Wee picked up the gun and smelled the barrel. He took a deep breath, he liked it. But he didn't smile. He just stared blankly at the commercial for the 5AM news.

"Police Hunt for Killer Child. Details first on FOX!"

Pee Wee took the gun and aimed at the TV holding the trigger tightly. "Puhggggg". He pretended.

Stephanie walked through the door passing Joanne.

"So who was that."

"That's Muhammad, from when I was a kid."

Joanne closed the door.

"Ain't that the nigger who walked out on you and Raheem?"

Stephanie had to smile, weakly.

"It wasn't quite like that Jo."

"That's what you said it was. He walked out didn't he?"

"Jo he wasn't really the father. Is that what you wanted to know."

"Hey I was just askin' who the nigger was."

"So why does he have to be a nigger? You were the one who said that was a bad word."

"Hey I'm just making conversation. You have a hard day today baby."

Joanne moved in with a strong arm of support. Stephanie braced herself into Jo's arm.

"Me and Muhammad are doing business. I'm organizing some buses for him. We did a lot of work today from LA to Birmingham."

"Look…"

There was a kiss to the temple.

"…That's why I'm here baby, for them hard days."

"I know Jo, I know."

This is when Joanne's other arm came into play. Still for Stephanie something was missing.

He had made his million dollars with Stephanie by his side. Who would of ever thunk it? In the space of one day he had made the biggest move of his life next to someone he had hated as no other. But Stephanie wasn't all that bad. At the age of 37 he realized that an ex-con was to a woman what a short skirted prostitute was to a man.: Pure raw sex. For sure if he had run across a short skirt at anytime in his life he would of abandoned all and jumped on it. Could he blame Stephanie for doing the same. Irregardless that was twenty years ago.

Tonight was big and there it was, the weed on the table. He had done it all, mission accomplished. This was the time to celebrate, why not enjoy a joint. The thought hit him that he wanted more. He wanted more than to be high. He wanted more than a two hour doze back into his twenty year old adolescence. For a few years he even equated reefer with being Black. It had dawned on him years earlier that Black culture only comes out of adolescence. Anything past music and sports was apt to be questioned. And once when he played Louis Armstrong all week on his tape deck at work he found out that even music has it's limits. This was part of the beauty of the Nation: Even if you didn't like them you admired the fact that it was an adult Negro institution created by Negroes from Negro culture. Louis had smoked weed until the day he died. He got a house in Queens while his manager got a block in Manhattan. Muhammad wanted more.

# A Land Far, Far Away: STAR WARS

It was now Wednesday, the 11th, five days away. After a good count Muhammad realized he had rented out the first 400 buses. 297 of them he sold at forty bucks a seat, 83 buses he sold at fifty and for twenty buses he got sixty dollars a seat. That alone grossed the better side of half a million. Plus there were the buses that Stephanie rented out which averaged a hundred bucks a seat. He wasn't sure but he believed they had rented out about 700 buses and they were buses that were rented to organizations and not individuals so the money would came in lump sums. Lump sums that would add up to $2,800,000. There was no need to call for his balance as he knew he could buy anything. He went direct to the bank and asked for help. He went to a downtown branch at 18th and Market. The first bank officer to approach him in the seating area was White. Muhammad politely shook him off and pointed to the Black bank officer, Rodney Burns. In his routine old blazer, blue jeans and Chuck Taylor sneaks he spoke quickly to the White banker and said that Mr. Burns was his friend and that he would wait. When Rodney Burns saw the plain Negro pointing his way, he frowned ever

*The Adventures of Muhammad Smith and The Million Man March*

so slightly and finished with the elderly Black woman and called to Muhammad pushing a smile through his contempt. Another late payment he figured. When Muhammad asked for his balance straight laced Burns thought it was a gimmick to explain why he was late. Punching the numbers into his terminal he excused himself from the desk with a sudden question on his face. Speaking to his White co-worker they walked back to his terminal and pushed a few more buttons.

"Do you have ID Mr. Smith?"

Charlie pulled out his license and answered the question of his Grandmother's maiden name, Brown. Meanwhile the White banker pushed more buttons.

"Rodney, these numbers are right."

The White guy spoke and there was no denying it.

"Mr. Smith your balance is two million, one hundred ninety six thousand, seven hundred forty nine dollars and sixty four cents...How can I help you sir?"

"First of all I want some privacy."

Muhammad looked to the White guy who got the hint and left.

"Now Mr. Burns I want you to learn the definition of respect and get rid of that routine Negro look."

"Excuse me Mr. Smith."

"What can I do with this money? You only insure to a hundred grand. Where do I put this kind of money?"

Taking a final look at his computer screen Burns takes a breath.

"Well many of our inheritances buy T-Bills for a few months or a year and then set up a trust."

"T-Bills?"

"Treasury notes, government bonds, not taxable but it only pays slightly less than inflation. And a trust can invest in more lucrative things like business, stocks or real estate and the tax rate is much lower than individual rates. With the year in T-Bills you have time to set up the trust anyway you want."

"Tell me more."

The two of them went at it for an hour with Burns making phone calls, opening new accounts and setting up the Bond purchase. On top of this Muhammad walked out of the bank with two cashier checks worth twenty five thousand each. He wanted some spending money. Just before he left Mr. Burns, in his $200 JC Penny suit, pulled Muhammad to the side.

"Hey brother, you going to the Million Man March?"

Muhammad made his way to his answering service who complained that people were still calling even though all the buses were gone. Muhammad asked where most of the calls were coming from and they told him New York. Muhammad instructed them to sell 50 more buses at seventy dollars a seat. With a quick call to Mercury Bus Incorporated the buses would be in place. Then the mail service told him that if these were tickets for a Monday event he would have to start using an overnight service. Taking their suggestion he called UPS and arranged a mass mailing at a buck fifty per envelope, guaranteed two day delivery, to include Sunday but since all but 2000 individual tickets were sold it would be a done deal by Friday. After lunch at the Down Town Restaurant, complete with baked fish, he made his way to Stephanie's office where she had almost all of the thousand buses rented out. Still there was work for him to do. He had to call, reserve and

*The Adventures of Muhammad Smith and The Million Man March*

verify the buses. Besides it was getting to be fun being with Stephanie. She seemed to enjoy it too. While there was no time in the office for the conversation they both wanted to have, after five they would enjoy dinner at Becky's on Fairmount Avenue. A Black restaurant that Stephanie's organization had helped to secure the initial loan.

"Hey girl, you ain't been down here for a minute."

"Hello Becky. This is an old friend, Muhammad Charles Smith, an entrepreneur who's taking forty thousand brothers to the Million Man March."

Stephanie was almost proud.

"Mr. Smith do you think a million men will go?"

"Easy. No problem. Everyday I get a phone call. Heck if I had bumped into Stephanie a week earlier, I'd be taking eighty thousand."

He was proud too.

"Listen Steph, dinner is on me. You and Mr. Smith enjoy the evening."

"Can I leave a tip?"

"Why yes Mr. Smith I think we can accommodate you and the little lady."

With that Becky left them with their menus. They could have anything they wanted.

"So what will it be Stephanie, grilled salmon or fresh Maine lobster at market prices?"

"Fresh. You haven't been fresh since the 11$^{th}$ grade Muhammad Charles. But now that you mention it I'll have the grilled salmon."

"So she was nice. Doesn't seem like the victims who come to the offices of ISIS. Is she a college friend?"

"Becky owned a hoagie shop over on Ridge. One day she hits the number for a hundred grand. Her car

*Anonymous*

was seven years old but her credit was shaky. We helped her get the loan for this place."

"With a hundred grand why did she need a loan? She could of had the best sandwich shop in North Philly."

"This place is growing Muhammad. Heck this use to be North Philly, now they call it the Art Museum area. She didn't want North Philly, she wanted more."

"I can really understand that. I really can. Besides I don't want to talk about business right now. I want to hear about you."

"Oh really. And just what do you want to know Mr. Smith?"

"The routine, like how come you're not married?"
She smiled.

"And I want to know what you're going to do with $400,000?"

"Four hundred thousand dollars and just where did that come from?"

"Ten dollars a seat, don't you remember that. Ten dollars times forty thousand. You do the math?"

She considered the sum, with a bit of reflection.

"Well, that's really the organizations money."

"Something tells me the director just got a raise."

They gave their order to the waitress and the food arrived, hot and steamy.

"So why aren't you married?"

The smile of money faded from her face.

"That's a hard question Muhammad. You know I could ask the same."

"…Ahhh, after 12$^{th}$ grade, love never was the same."

"Yeah something like that happened to me too…"

*The Adventures of Muhammad Smith and The Million Man March*

Dinner continued with local talk like the kid who shot his teacher or national issues like how the Democrats were taking a beating in every election since last November. No way Clinton was winning next year. Fine black president he turned out to be. They spoke briefly of Raheem. They were both proud of him but every mention of his name seemed to have a stinging effect deep within them both.

They left with Becky walking them to the door. When she returned to the table, she was overwhelmed by the five one hundred dollar bills on the table. The drive to Stephanie's home was routine until the end. Almost at Mt. Airy Street and one turn away, Muhammad stayed on Germantown Avenue and started to ramble.

"I use to like taking the trolley up to Jenks. All the way to Chestnut Hill. The 23 all the way to the end of Germantown Ave...I use to want to live up here, heck I still do, but two weeks ago I couldn't mortgage a house past West Philly."

At Mermaid Lane in front of the Deaf School he parked the car. The wide estate of the school gave a certain romance to his rambling.

"Heck the worst day was when Keith challenged me to a fight and I backed down. Yep, skinny old Keith. But I wanted to be a part of Chestnut Hill or even Upper Mt. Airy. I wanted to belong to something, someone, anything. You know on some nights just anything. But it never was like that. The world don't work that way.

She was silent listening to his strange logic. She only looked out at the cobblestones, cement and the lush green grasses of the School for the Deaf.

"That's what everybody say, the world don't work that way. Upper Mt. Airy is far beyond my grasp. It don't belong to me. You know, you were never mine. I wanted to belong to you. Since really the couch, I wanted to belong to you…I know, I know you got other plans, you got your own life and all that but I'm sorry that I ran off like that. I just wanted to…"

She took his chin by her finger tips and turned to kiss him. As her fingers rolled across his face her hand held him dear. For him there was no resistance. With purpose he felt her waist pushing towards him. He took the whole of her back within his arms then drove his hand to her thigh as she held his lips ever closer. Pushing the arm rest out of the way he completed his embrace as her arms tightened their hold. And then, for a moment,

they pushed against each other as if wild dogs. But the moment passed and his fingers found the lever and the seat glided into a reclining position. Still she said nothing for her lips were engulfed in a strange rapture that held to the effort of sucking every once of pleasure from this man's lips. He broke away to bite into her neck as she allowed herself only a moan so as not to scream. He held her face, her waist, everything he could think to touch he held dearly and oh how she followed.

It would be a memory for them both, a final balance to the memory of Raheem and the past.

********

He enjoyed every minute with Stephanie but the next morning the feelings were too strong. Today was Thursday. The buses from LA would be leaving the next day. Everything was in motion so Muhammad decided to do the same with his money. With his checkbook

*The Adventures of Muhammad Smith and The Million Man March*

he visited fifteen different banks and opened fifteen different bank accounts. It was much the same at every bank. He wrote the check in front of the banker for one hundred thousand dollars. The banker would all but laugh in his face, walk away to check at another computer and then came back with the smile wiped off of their faces. It was nice having fifteen different people in suits really, really suck up to you. Now, in a strong sense, his money was insured. He arranged an appointment with a corporate lawyer who was also a CPA. As luck would have it, it turned out to be an educated Black man. Charlie was very careful and was slightly put off when this guy tried to get him to sign a pre-printed contract. All Muhammad wanted to know was what was the best format for a trust fund and what was the difference in a good trust fund and a bad trust fund. The guy told him about revocable and irrevocable and various combinations. The magic of partnerships and the simple gimmick of incorporation. Charlie asked him about stocks. The lawyer reminded him about 1987. When Charlie told him about just putting his money in T-Bills for a few months the lawyer tried everything he knew to belittle the petty return on bonds. Now was the time to sign the contract he insisted. Charlie stuck to his guns and just wanted to know about trust funds. There were living trusts and the kind that came into effect when you died. The lawyer assured him that he wanted the living kind. The guy told him that most lottery winners blew it from the get go when they signed the ticket. The wise move would be to put the ticket into the name of a trust that you're the president of. A trust or a corporation, sometimes they both work the lawyer said. All that Muhammad needed to do was to trust him with his money. The lawyer's office was very nice but Muhammad was keeping his money. He did take the guy's card and promised to call.

Already it was two in the afternoon. Two weeks ago he would be at work hoping to make his Cadillac payment…Two week ago, two weeks ago. That was so…two weeks ago. Things were different now. Now he felt a surge of confidence, his options were multiplied beyond his wildest dreams. Before he knew it he was on the Amtrak Metroliner to New York. By five he was in time to see rush hour in New York City. Like a wave, commuters rushed into Penn Station as he was leaving. He felt a chill in the air and stopped into Macy's to buy an overcoat and a cute pair of gloves. He asked the cabbie to take him to the richest part of town and the cabbie took him to Times Square. It had been a while since he felt the thrill of bright lights.

He ate at the Howard Johnson on Broadway before he realized that it was just a tad below the quality of a decent tourist trap and the burgers were still five dollars. Still he ate well and walked north on Broadway passing a sea of people ranging from the chic to the cheap but the street itself was electric. This was all his. He walked the streets of New York City lost without a clue ending up at "Bessie Smiths" lounge. It was so obvious through the wide front window that this was the culture that would be his life. Walking through the glass doors, he felt a certain cockiness that he had more money than anybody in the joint. Then he saw Bill Cosby at a table in the rear. He stepped to the bar and asked for Champaign. The barmaid said with such grace that a glass was twenty dollars and the bottle a hundred eighty five. He took the bottle and told the

*The Adventures of Muhammad Smith and The Million Man March*

barmaid to give a glass to the girl three seats down... Her name would be Sandy. After the second glass he asked what was the best hotel in town. She said the Bellevue Stratford on Park Avenue. On the third drink her dark, dark skin seemed to shine with every drop. When he asked for directions to the hotel Sandy showed him the way. This wasn't Kansas.

The next morning he gave her cab fare and they were happy with a kiss and never saw each other again. It was almost 7:30AM and in about four hours buses would be rolling from Los Angeles. He called his main account for the almost final total that was now distributed over maybe twenty different accounts and banks.

"On October Thirteenth your available balance is Nine Hundred Forty Three Thousand Six Hundred Nineteen Dollars And Sixty Four Cents".

He took Amtrak back to Philly, first class. With the "Metro Phone" he called Stephanie.

"Muhammad where have you been boy. I been looking all over the place for you."

"I'm sorry Steph, just a old habit. A got a touch of solitude in New York."

"New York City?"

"Yep, I went to New York City. I wanted to see how the rich half lives. I even saw Bill Cosby."

"You mean in person?"

"I mean in person."

"You know the buses left from San Francisco."

"Already? I completely forgot about San Francisco."

"Mac, what's that noise?"

*Anonymous*

"It's a train Stephanie, I'm calling you from a train."

"So you livin' large."

"So how's it going, did you get any calls, any problems?"

"No Muhammad. The Gay Mans Alliance is the most orderly group I deal with. Besides they can't wait to see a million Black men."

"Listen I'll be there as soon as I get off the train."

"Mac?"

"Yeah Stephanie."

"Thanks for the other night."

"All praise due Allah."

He hung up.

Once in Philly, and with Stephanie, Muhammad could do little more than sit back and watch. Stephanie had taken over the tedious logistics that would of challenged him, at best. She loved it, in fact it was part of her job description, organizing trips to Harrisburg and Washington. The trips to Harrisburg, the Pennsylvania state capital, were local affairs that her and her "Women's Lib" group from Philly would go to lobby and beg. And the trips to Washington were planned regionally with groups from New York, Ohio and Atlanta. Yet on all of these trips there was rarely unity. Everyone had their own agenda: PUP in Philly, The Philadelphia Unemployment Project, could never see much more than extending unemployment benefits. The Atlanta branch of the NAACP always complained that no one ever went to their annual Martin Luther King dinner, held in April. Often it was a challenge getting many of these groups in the same room, much less the same bus. But Stephanie mentioned that this trip was much easier. Even though there were many more people they all wanted the same thing: Direction.

It was only the second time she had coordinated a national trip. Ironically her first organized event was a national effort that also gave birth to I.S.I.S. She had conceived of I.S.I.S. and a national trip to change the Rape Victim Disclosure law both in the same afternoon ten years earlier when she was doing volunteer work at the Women's Shelter on Arch Street. It could also be said that this was her first "man" event. She liked it. It was the first time that so many men were asking her what to do and not trying to get at her panties. When the scoutmaster for the Black Boy Scouts in Pittsburgh called she was struck at the erectness she noticed in his voice and having Muhammad behind her stirred nostalgic memories. He could only listen as she so carelessly told the scout guy that a representative from the Negro Council of Negro Women would be on each bus and that all he had to do was be at the parking lot of Three River Stadium early on Monday morning. After Pittsburgh there was the Ardmore Africans from Oklahoma. They only had one bus but wanted another at the last minute. Stephanie reminded them their bus would be leaving the next day from Ardmore High School then she put them on hold. Muhammad made a call to Mr. Peters and arranged to get a bus to Oklahoma from a depot in Dallas. Stephanie picked up the phone and told them they could have the bus but the money had to be in the account by 5 o'clock. Next it was Vermont. Their only problem was they couldn't find enough Black people and wanted their money back. She put them on hold and talked it over with Muhammad. Picking up the phone she told Vermont

*Anonymous*

they could get back 25% of their money but they had to take on some people from Harlem. When she said Harlem, Vermont put her on hold. A short time later they came back and said ok. She was in her element.

*********

Merion Berry's government in DC was struggling to complete the logistics of what now appeared to be the arrival of one million men. No one had predicted that a million men were actually coming. But on this Friday before the Monday, Mayor Berry was in the midst of a last minute rush to plan street closures, prevent gridlock and request two hundred National Guardsmen to supplement police officers who would be doing traffic duty. "We've done this before. A lot of people come here all the time. This is nothing new for us. We'll be ready." Still all sides wondered if the city would be ready. Everything from toilets to red lights had to be planned. And with each passing moment black men across America were changing their mind and coming to the Million Man March. Even Albert Wynn, a local congressman from Baltimore, had changed his mind but yesterday to go to the Million Man March. For many Black politicians with local White constituencies it made no political sense to say anything about the march at all. Still there were those like Rev. Joseph Lowery of the SCLC, who also had publicly changed his mind to go to the March. Leaders of his ilk suddenly realized not only the grass roots appeal of the Million Man March, they also saw the possibility of history passing them by. All of a sudden a million Black Men felt the need to say that they were

Black. Mort Sahl, a comedian ran a steady joke for almost 10 years now and Muhammad got a hoot every time he heard it. Mort a White man who looked like a Jew would say, in his comedy routine, "Oh I didn't even notice you were Black." This was the state of race relations in America. OJ is noticed, Rodney King is noticed and on the words of White trash in Alabama every black man in Alabama is noticed, but the official line was not to notice. Day by day Black men to include doctors and the homeless began to think that Louis Farrakhan would be noticed.

\*\*\*\*\*\*\*\*

Louis Eugene Walcott, born in America in 1933 to a mother who was born in St. Kitts of the British Caribbean. In 1949 he appeared on the Ted Mack Amateur Hour playing a violin and quickly learned how to play a crowd. His music went on to the point where he made several records in the Calypso style of the day. 'Calypso Gene' perhaps would have had a national stage if not for Harry Belefonte. In those days of the 50's there could only be one Negro in any given situation from the star of a Basketball team to an actor in a movie, there could only be one Negro and in 1955 Calypso Gene was not the one. This is when he joined the Muslims. His music career continued until the release of his recording of "A Black Man's heaven is a White Man's Hell". His Muslim friends liked it though it didn't do well on the Billboard Top Ten.

Meanwhile the same mass media that, perhaps, gave birth to the civil rights movement was catching on to the Million Man thing, even the Black media.

Much of the Black print media was strongly associated with the Baptist Church, which had rejected the march on several fronts. The religious difference of Christian/Muslim was the least of these reasons. Only Black radio and TV paid any real attention to the march. Yet not even they could get an interview with Louis Farrakhan. Once the White media stopped thinking about OJ Simpson and a million black men in one place they began to consider the organizers of the event. They began to wonder about the Black Muslims. Meanwhile the Black media, who knew to call them the Nation of Islam, portrayed the march as a "finding of self", a first united step towards the goal of a national unity that only Jews seemed to of accomplished on a global scale. As all White people across America braced themselves for a million black men in one place at the same time, Black people longed to tell White people that they were White. As they come with their timid dance steps into all aspects of American Negro culture it was hard to tell little Johnny that he was a white boy, in a serious way. Yet as Black Americans took brave steps into White culture they were measured carefully with the yardstick of silky hair. Never daring to say or display that they were in fact Black. The skin color was enough.

White establishments not only in Washington, but all along the corridors of I-95 and all roads west, began to make plans to close their shops and offices as it became more evident that a lot of Black folks were coming to town and they weren't little old ladies. In fact there were more stores closed on the 16th in Washington DC than there was for George Washington's Birthday.

Real or imagined how could a million Black men fit into anyone's theory of perfection.

Black establishments seemed to coalesce with an energy not seen since 1968. Black mom and pops seemed to enjoy a spike in "buy Blackness" that was springing up spontaneously everywhere. Black merchandisers were selling everything from Million Man T-shirts (One or two of which had stolen Muhammad's poster design) to old velvet pictures of MLK that had been stored away in the basement. The one question that was dominant in every Black community, African American church, ghetto street corner and Negro farm east of the Mississippi, the one question that was everywhere was "Are you going to the Million Man March?" CNN could only grasp at it's meaning.

********

He had the evening completely planned out. First they would do dinner at the Down Town. Then he had tickets to the Merriam Theater where they were doing some Black play of which he himself had never heard of but he figured Stephanie would be impressed. He even had the hotel suite, with a bottle of Champaign, at what he still liked to call the Hershey Hotel at Broad and Locust Streets. They were going to have a wonderful night. It was planned. Then at 5 o'clock before he could say "dinner at Tiffany's" she told him that she had to go home. He tried to say "but" and slide a arm but she only pushed him away.

"Not now. Not this fast Muhammad."

"Come on Stephanie. It'll be fun."

He went for a kiss but she turned her head.

"I can't go there Mac. Stop it."
"So is this a Joanne thing?"
"Muhammad, don't talk about my personal life."

This definitely broke the mood. His arm slid back to it's original position.

"My mistake."

He was in full retreat.

"Look it's not that I don't like you. It's just that I got too much on my mind right now. I'm taking the R7 home. You can use the back office if you want, Mrs. Harris closes up at six. I'll probably call you tomorrow and definitely on Sunday. We have a lot of work to do"

She grabbed her bag, her sweater and left. Kinda sudden. He didn't need a back office he needed a good stiff drink. Finally he left B&B's from 15th and South at about 11 o'clock that night. It was time to go home. Maybe he could catch "Star Wars" on HBO.

Across town Pee Wee beat the odds of a city wide search and lounged at home in front of his new TV. He was mesmerized by all of the channels he had on the cable TV he had brought with is new found wealth. CNN and the local news meant nothing compared to HBO at 11 o'clock on a Friday night. For tonight though it was the Fresh Prince of Belaire. It was the show where Will got the girl and Carl got stuck taking out the thrash. In the eyes of an illiterate, juvenile murderer this was even better than naked women on Showtime. He barely had a clue that anyone was looking for him. Fact is he barely had any clue beyond the gun in his hand and the comforts of home. Trash littered his room as it did throughout the house his mother had somehow claimed as hers. Perhaps TV would offer him a clue, perhaps he

*The Adventures of Muhammad Smith and The Million Man March*

was more like Carl and got stuck with the trash. All he had to do now was take it out. Then he turned to HBO in the middle of Star Wars. He was amazed by the ease at which Luke Skywalker could kill with the light saber. And in the remaining moments of the movie Pee Wee found justification in any act of violence that took place. In fact the only responsibility he could see in this mythical tale was the responsibility to kill.

"PEE WEE." His mother called.

"Yeah ma."

"I got some chicken wings you want some?"

"I got some potato chips from the Chinese store. I'm alright."

He turned up the volume on the TV, the black guy was about to kill somebody. It was classic.

Tonight Stevie was in New York. He was just getting on the Jersey Turnpike as Muhammad was arriving in Philly on Amtrak that morning. His destination was Spanish Harlem above 125$^{th}$ Street but he had time so he brought along some chick who was just young enough to shut up, lay down and enjoy the shoes from Macy's. They checked into a nice hotel room in midtown Manhattan, enjoyed a quickie and then caught a movie on Broadway. Still it was daylight, these Ricans liked to do business at night so he let her have her way at Macy's and Saks 5$^{th}$ Avenue. She seemed to like the shopping bags more than the clothes they held. It didn't matter, when she got back to the hotel room they did another quickie. After some weed and a few lines of coke it was finally dark enough. He showered, cologned, and wore his black suit, black shirt with a gold necklace. From a small box he pulled out a gold tooth cap and put it into place, his right front tooth. Looking to the mirror he smiled then flashed his jacket to look at the 9mm he kept in his belt. From his pocket he reached for the bankroll of hundred dollar bills. He just smelled it and put it back in his pocket.

"Give me some sugar baby."

She got off the bed with her robe flowing openly. Pressing her flesh to his side he admired the sight and leaned just a bit for the young girl to kiss his cheek.

"Take care of yourself Boo."

She turned on the television in time to see Darth Vader's dispatch of an idiot.

In less than an hour he was in the heart of the barrio of 137th Street in the fourth floor apartment of a gray haired Dominican named Jose. Jose had young children who ran about playing to the beat of salsa music while Jose's nephew stood behind the seated Stevie with a shotgun.

"Why all the heat Jose? You know me. I'm your ace boon coon."

"This is a big order my friend, I don't like surprises. What's the occasion, if you don't mind me asking?"

"I got a new customer, a white boy."

"This white boy vato, you know him well si?"

"Yeah I know the nigger, why you so worried. It's my butt on the line."

"Si Senor. We don't sell to White boys amigo. It's a good ground rule. Maybe you should take this cocaine and find some nice Black people to sell to, cops give you no problem. You sell to White boys vato and their mothers start to make noise talking about the evils of the world. Too many cops vato"

"Jose I been sellin' dope since before you got off the boat nigger. I don't need no pep talk. Here the money now where the dope?"

"Si Senor, the dope."

********

Raheem, at first glance was beyond Black. With his dread locks, that were just becoming fashionable, and the loose clothes he wore he could easily fit the description for half a dozen crimes in North Philly on any given night. But tonight he was in the manicured South Philly apartment of Timothy, a nice beefy, blond white boy he had met in school. They liked listening to Old Jazz and Blues as they sipped alcohol in all it's varieties. Timothy brought the drinks to Raheem on the couch, clicked off the television and took a seat beside him.

"That's my mom's favorite movie"

"Tsk, tsk. So what did you do today?"

"I was with my mom, at her office. She's trying to hook up this million man thing with some guy named Muhammad."

"What is that million man thing about any way? I mean what are they going to do, like have a big riot or something?"

"I don't know Tim. The Muslims I've seen ain't about riots. I never knew them but I see them from time to time. They ain't about that."

"So what do these 'Muslims' do, pray to Allah or God or something?"

"I really don't know. The same thing as all churches do I suppose."

"All churches don't gather a million black men in one place."

"Oh."

"Sooooo?"

"So…what?"

"What are all those Black guys going to do on Monday?"

"I don't know."

"Well aren't you going?"

"No. I'm not going to the Million Man March."

"I thought it was a Black thing."

"I don't want to be Black I'm a human being."

"Not with a whopper like you got."

"So now it's the whopper thing."

"Whatever."

"Did you hear about that teacher? You know they still haven't found that kid."

"Yeah, I heard."

"Such animals I swear. I know it sounds bad Raheem but the cops should just go through North Philly and clean all those people out. It would be an improvement for everybody.

Raheem slid back resting his head on the couch and just stared.

"What are you thinking about Mr. Human being?"

"It wasn't North Philly Timothy, it happened in West Philly."

"Oh you know what I mean."

"Yeah you mean West Philly too. See it's talk like that Timothy that give people like Farrakhan credibility."

"Who is this Farrakhan?"

"He's the leader of the Muslims."

"I thought Malcolm X was the leader. He's the only one I see on TV. Him and Ali."

"Malcolm X is dead Timothy. Some guys from Newark, NJ shot him in New York. Guess where Farrakhan was?"

"He lives in Chicago, doesn't he?"

"Farrakhan was in Newark. That's what my grandfather told me: Louis Farrakhan was in Newark."

"Oh, well that's ominous. But that 'Plymouth Rock' thing that Malcolm X says is so cute. Does Farrakhan say stuff like that?"

Still deep in thought Raheem slowly speaks.

"I've only heard him speak once or twice. One thing I can say, he don't like White people."

"So is that what's he's going to say on Monday on National TV 'I don't like White People?' My God won't that be boring."

Raheem just sat with his head leaned back, still in thought.

"Lover you're thinking far too much. Come here."

With that Timothy took Raheem's cheek into his palm and kissed him. It was a welcome change of subject.

\*\*\*\*\*\*\*\*

Joanne's head lay in her lap, snoring. It was her worst trait. In the dark living room Stephanie looked to the TV. It was Star Wars, her favorite movie of all time. She wasn't sure what it was but she fancied the thought that it was the obvious romance between Luke and Princess Leia. As they swung across the great traverse

*Anonymous*

she waited for him to take her in his arms and kiss her. Then with a loud grunt from Joanne, Stephanie looked down with no smile and an intensity in her stare. Joanne kept on snoring and Stephanie kept on looking. How did it come to this? With a pillow from the couch Stephanie gently placed it beneath Joanne's head as she rose from the couch and sat in the chair nearby. She never told anyone that she liked Star Wars. It seemed so childish, so violent, so White. When asked such questions she would usually say "The Color Purple" or if she really wanted to get metaphysical she would say the "Emperor Jones" with Paul Robeson. Perhaps the greatest Black Man in the first half of the 20$^{th}$ Century, who died silently at 4949 Walnut Street in Philadelphia during her lifetime. She could clearly remember that his death garnered little more than a large paragraph in the local paper. But she rarely got that deep. In all reality, this was the flick for her. From it's very beginning the massive words on the screen, that told a story that was a movie in and of itself. And then, the battle to save the queen! It was all so gothic. And this especially, she never told anyone, she thought that Darth Vader was the sexiest man alive. Even against the magnificent Peter Cushing, Lord Vader stood tall. Stephanie took a gander to Joanne on the couch and then off into space. For no special reason at all a tear fell from her cheek.

Then the end came with Luke Skywalker in victory over all except Darth Vader. The sequels were nice but there was nothing like the original. With that in mind she woke Joanne up.

"Joe, Joe wake up."

Joanne jerked to attention and then just as quick knew it was a wake up call.

*The Adventures of Muhammad Smith and The Million Man March*

"What time is it?"

"It's almost twelve. Come on Joanne your bleeding, you'll mess up the couch."

"Was I snoring?"

She rose to her feet giving her body a long, stretching yawn.

"No. Come on let's go to bed. I'll meet you up there."

Stephanie casually went barefoot up the steps and into the bedroom. Pulling off her shirt she just sat on the edge of the bed and stared to the floor. It was a blank look as if nothing was inside of her. But there it was again, the tear on the cheek.

"Stephanie What's wrong"

It was Joanne! Stephanie quickly wiped the tear and said.

"Nothing."

She stood and took off her jeans in a hurried yet natural way that subtlety gave her time to hide her feelings. Soon they were beneath the covers and the lights were out.

"You mind if I turn on the news?"

"No, not at all. Just keep it low, like you always do." Stephanie said.

"News: Two, three four times a day: KYW news radio 1060…..Police are still looking for the child who shot and killed his third grade teacher in West Philadelphia on Monday. Here's Susan Thomas from the Round House in Center City.

"Yes Sam, police can only admit embarrassment at a child run amok. Here's Detective Ronald Jenkins of the homicide unit.

*Anonymous*

"This is an amazing case, I'll be the first to admit it Susan. Here we have a child who is assigned to a class but since he changed his name two years ago and has moved a half a dozen times since that, all records of his identity are worthless. We do know that he was born Jihad Al-Maleek. But the child and his parents seemed to of adopted a new name. The best we can come up with is Pee Wee. So we're asking for the community's help in solving this horrible crime. It's the most despicable thing I've seen in my 18 years on the force."

"There you have it Sam: Beware of a child known as Pee Wee, a young Black male."

"Thank you Susan. And now for sports......"

"A Black male. Did you hear that?" Joe asked.

"Yeah, so what?"

"Why are our brothers so worthless?"

"And we're the saints?"

"KYW news time at the tone will be 12 o'clock midnight."

# Girls Were Girls, Men Were Men: ALL IN THE FAMILY

Saturday started with a phone call. It was James. Muhammad struggled for the phone in the middle of a dream with reluctant determination.

"Hello……..Who is this?"

"Charlie it's me, James."

"James, cousin James. Cousin James what time is it?"

"It's six thirty on the dot. I've been waiting to call you."

"At six AM? Well I guess this is going to be good."

Muhammad sat up on the side of his bed.

"You still doing this bus thing to the Million Man March?"

"Yeah I got a few buses going down that way on Monday. Why?"

"Me and my club we've decided to go as a team but we can't find a bus. So then I thought about you."

"Well first of all cuz it'll cost you two grand. Second of all, what kind of club you belong to that want to go to the Million Man March?"

*Anonymous*

"The Montgomery County League of Negro Republicans."

"The Montgomery County League of Super Heroes…Really?"

"Charlie I only meant this as a business proposition. There's no need for any personal stuff."

"Personal! James three weeks ago you were calling me stupid for even thinking about the Million Man March. Now you want a bus for the Black Republicans of Suburban America! I mean Excuuuuse me. Just what is it that you and these Negro republicans hope to find at the Million Man March, a tax write off?"

"Fair question cousin but the best that I can tell you is that I want to hear what he is going to say. I'm hoping he can say what I've never heard before."

"And what would that be Cousin James?"

"God why did you make me Black?"

There were a half a dozen ways to Sunday that Muhammad could of answered that question. Each one of them were nasty and vindictive along the lines of calling someone an Uncle Tom but Muhammad remained silent.

"Tell you what James you can have a bus at the original rate of 1,600."

"Are we being nice? Showing care and/or responsibility? This is a surprise."

"Hey James."

"Yes Charlie."

"Don't make me change my mind."

"No I take you at your word Charlie, you never were a liar. I've always liked that about you."

"You seen Grandmom lately?"

"Yesterday as a matter of fact. She tells me you're doing quite well and she brags that you paid her back all of the money with interest."

"You know Grandmom."

"So tell me Charlie, how is it going."

"Do you know anything about trust funds? Some banker guy says that's the way to go."

"Trust funds, so you did hit a home run."

"How much is 5% on an annual basis on a principle of a million dollars, times two."

"Looks like Aunt Sally isn't the only one who brags."

"Hey what is family for?"

With that Muhammad's day began. Two days away from zero hour when all buses would be in route to Washington DC. He showered and dressed in his $200 pants, $100 shirt and $50 underwear. All brand new from Boyd's. Brushing his fade he took one look in the mirror and then turned to the phone. At 7:30 it was still early but he had one call he had to make. He reached for the phone, but it rang first.

"Hello?"

"Muhammad I'm sorry. I'm sorry please forgive me. It was all my fault Muhammad, I was so wrong. Please forgive me."

"Stephanie?"

"Yes Muhammad, whatever you want. Whatever you want Muhammad I was such a fool. You were the one Muhammad. You were always the one. Whatever you want Muhammad. I have so much to makeup for."

"Stephanie, slow down girl. You don't owe me nothing. That other day, at the seafood place, you said I was an old lost friend. Stephanie with you by my side we'll never be old, we'll never be lost. We've always been friends Stephanie."

"Mac I want to see you today. I have to see you today."

"Well shouldn't we be at the office today. I mean after all there's bound to be a ton of calls."

"Mac, I don't want to do business today."

"Come now what would Mrs. O'Donald say from the fourth grade…"

"I remember 'business before pleasure'. Muhammad?"

"Yes Stephanie."

"I love you. You hear me boy, I love you."

"Be there for me Steph. Be there for me. I know that sounds selfish but…"

"No Muhammad it's not selfish at all. It would be selfish only not to give you what you should of had a long time ago."

"Stephanie, don't worry about the past. I've forgotten about it many years ago."

He lied but the moment was special.

"Am I going to see you today Muhammad?"

"Let's meet at the office at about 9 o'clock."

"I'm sorry Muhammad."

"Stephanie. Forget it. Be there."

He got a nice breakfast of chipped beef and home fries at the Down Town restaurant. Then he walked to 1201 Chestnut, Stephanie's building. Not seeing her he went up to the 7th floor and waited. He didn't wait long. On the next elevator right behind his she arrived.

"Hope you weren't waiting long. The R7 was late again."

"No I just got here."

*The Adventures of Muhammad Smith and The Million Man March*

The phone could be heard through the door. She rushed past him with key in hand and unlocked the door. Then she turned to his lips and kissed him.

"I love you Mac."

Then she went into the office, but not to the phone. With Muhammad behind her she turned, embraced him and kissed. He was overcome but soon followed suit with an embrace of his own. But before a head of steam could be built a second phone rang and then a third. This was surely going to be a busy day.

Much of it was the routine, like where to catch the bus and should food be brought. Some of the calls though were more serious in nature and most of those were from all the independent bus companies Muhammad had hired before he got the Mercury contract. Some insisted the trip was too dangerous and refused to go. Muhammad told them he had a contract and Stephanie, an old pro with bus trips to Washington, dropped the names of local lawyers she knew and the bus owners knew. Still the Black Boy Scouts from Pittsburgh had a complaint. Well not a complaint really but a demand. They demanded they be allowed to go to the bathroom at least once an hour and wanted to verify their bus had a toilet on board, which it did. They called right back wanting to know if they could spray disinfectant on the bus. They got a laugh out of that one. The calls didn't slow down until about three that afternoon. All the while Stephanie had eyes. And with a five minute restbit from the phones she made her move. With Muhammad sitting at the side of her desk she asked him to look at a schedule for a bus route. He looked at the sheet of paper and explained that as long as the bus left on time there should be no problem.

"Yes Muhammad."

"The guy from Mercury told me that leaving early would eliminate a lot of that."

"Yes Muhammad."

She moved closer, for the obvious.

"But I am worried about the independents."

"Yes Muhammad."

"As a matter of fact I should of put it in the contract."

"Yes Muhammad."

"Stephanie you give me the willies when you…"

She didn't wait any longer. In an awkward way she stood and leaned forward until her lips met his and then lifted him up from his chair and wrapped her arms around his neck. It was an arm lock the likes of which Hulk Hogan had never seen. Muhammad had no choice but to hold her at the waist. This is when the phone rang. Muhammad took a look at the phone with an open eye. Stephanie responded by taking her leg and kicking the phone off of the desk. She pulled at Muhammad's neck until his body had her against the desk at hip level. Just what she wanted. When he finally pulled her closer to him her jeans spread wider and she started at his neck. He was getting the idea and soon found his hand beneath her blouse searching for the snap on her bra. But with one motion she had her blouse off and cleared off the clutter from the desk and crashing to the floor. He tried to be as fast with his shirt but the buttons got in the way. Stephanie didn't have this problem and merely ripped the buttons away and off at his arms. And on the upswing she grabbed his undershirt for his naked chest which she wanted so much on top of hers. Only the bra remained but she made that go away too and then they were kissing. It was more than a passion, it was a history of love lost and now tasted and by the way her mouth was working she was going for every drop. She wanted to feel every inch of his back in every way, almost probing for it's every strength. He soon found himself a slave to the gentle kindness he found awaiting him upon the soft caress of her chest and soon could not resist the pressure to mash them against him. She went for his pants, he her jeans. Fumbling with the belt she soon found her mark as did he with her kicking off her sneakers her leg found it's way free of her jeans and there she stood half dressed and ready. At first it was enough to just hold each other but soon, very soon, that was not enough and she took him into her gently but he gave a sudden push and she knew it was good when on the very next thrust there hips slammed into one another making sounds which could only be called animal at best. They bit at each other with their bodies in full motion. Still they held each other in a death grip until her back was flat on the desk and he supported himself with his arms. Now his whole body, from his knees to his shoulders, was one machine that pumped deep into her, deeper and deeper. She cried out, but not for mercy. Her legs, one still with jeans, crouched upward as the only thought on her mind was more.

Muhammad had never felt like this. This was better than before and with all his strength his face strained to give her more without regard as to whether the violent thrusts he was delivering to this soft mound of flesh was causing harm or joy. But for his own joy his arms bent and his head sank into her lips and he kissed her and her warm tongue. Suddenly the urge hit to stop humping and to start grinding. This was good, she was grinding back. Finding his way back to her breasts he kissed at her neck with his hips still out of control, pounding into the welcome of her thighs. Her moans were understood but they were not English. They were joy, understood in every language known to man. His moans were of a determination to push every thing he had into her soft, soft body. Then in a flurry he grabbed behind her hips and squeezed just as he penetrated her at a furious, intense and hard pace. She held him tight and with one final push she finally spoke.

"Thank you Muhammad."

He needed a new shirt and they decided it would be best if he walked out by himself and they would meet in the Gallery mall in twenty minutes, just enough time for him to buy a shirt. They took a cab to the Art Museum, one of their favorites as children, and laughed the evening away. Then for laughs they went to the Le Bec Fin on Walnut Street, the only five star restaurant in Philadelphia. The Maitre'D refused to let Stephanie come in with jeans so they went to Becky's on Fairmount Avenue. Becky was more than happy to see the biggest tip she had ever or ever would see in her life. What really caught Becky's eye was the fact that they were walking hand in hand. She gave them seats with a perfect view and a bottle of Champaign on the house. They took their respective turns at the rest rooms beside the register. They had a certain musk about them and both of them wanted to freshen up for whatever was next.

********

*The Adventures of Muhammad Smith and The Million Man March*

Stevie called Larry from the payphone on 63rd street. What he thought was a smart move was compromised long ago by the FBI. They listened closely.

"This Larry...Larry man it's me Stevie. You got the cash?"

"Ninety grand, like we agreed. You got the stuff?"

"Hey who you talkin' to nigger? You just be at your bar on Fairmount on Tuesday afternoon with the money."

"Why Tuseday, why not today?"

"Don't rush me man. Gots to do things proper, on a weekday, low profile."

"So why not Monday. Listen I got a ton of business here."

"It'll wait, besides I'm going to the Million Man March. It's a black thing you wouldn't know nothing about it."

"I thought that was like a anti-drug thing. You ain't gonna cop out on me, now are you brother?"

"Tuesday afternoon at two o'clock. Watch out."

"Alright Stevie, I'll be waiting."

"Yeah, we'll be waiting alright." The FBI agent said.

Now it was six forty-five AM on Sunday and yet again the phone. He was going to have to do something about this phone.

"Yeah, Hello...James?"

"Good Morning Charlie. It's been a long time since I woke you up."

"Grandmom, Grandmom."

225

Now he was awoke, but that was no reason to get out of bed.

"What brings you to my phone so early in the morning Grandmom?"

"You're taking a long trip tomorrow and I want you to come to church with me today."

"But Grandmom I went last week."

"No young man you met me at the church to take care of business. I want you to come with me today to listen to the lord."

"Oh, so now it's a God thing."

"I expect your car at my door at 10:30 young man."

"Yes mam."

His answer was slow, but obedient.

He wore the same suit but with a slightly more conservative twist. Today he wore a white shirt with a cheap, but clean, black tie from his old job at Fast Food Delite. It had dawned on him that perhaps he was getting a bit too fancy. Let's say 'too big for his britches'. The trip to New York was nice but Philly was home. Yeah he had money but no need to change the tune now. Oh the neighborhood would definitely have to go. There was no make believe to that. The people here in his slice of West Philly had become too desperate. People were getting shot for the pride and honor of a cigarette. And as in the Cambodian jungles of the late 70's people were shot just for appearing to be intellectual and thus by street definition, weak. Funny how the ghetto could be a jungle sometime.

He picked his grandmother up, a tad late, from the familiar 9th and Christian Street and escorted her to his Cadillac. He still took a certain pride in this car and

*The Adventures of Muhammad Smith and The Million Man March*

was still undecided if he would take his $2,000,000 and buy a new car or just get the AC fixed. Once his grandmother was in the car there returned a feeling of trust, love and companionship sometimes known as family.

"Grandmom, I'm rich. I got two million dollars in 15 different bank accounts."

Bam just like that he said it. She thought on it a while with the same smile she had when he knocked on her door.

"Your brother needs a good lawyer."

"I talked to him a few days ago. The subject did come up. Do you want to move Grandmom?"

"No, I been here all my life. If I move now I might get lost. But I wants to travel though. See my sister in Carolina and maybe even see Disney World."

"I thought you didn't like Disney. Said it was too white."

"It is, but even White people got their beauty too."

"Humph…What do you think of the march?"

"Oh I don't know. Can't get much worse than it is now."

"Look at them Rawandans over in Africa. They got it pretty bad."

"Yes, but they don't have Mickey Mouse."

Church was the usual, yet the familiar. From the days that his grandmother made him go he knew all the pleasantries that would proceed, with the old lady in the newest dress making the grandest hello. Today that lady was his grandmother.

"Sister Wallace, have you met my grandson?"

Sister Wallace had the newest clothes last week.

*Anonymous*

"This ain't the same Charlie Smith that use to sing in the Children's Choir. Why I know him from over at the Fast Food Delite near Fairmount. That your grandson. Why, I sees him over there all the time. Why young man if I ain't mistaken, I placed my order for a burger and fries with you but two weeks ago."

"That was my nephew James. Charlie is an entrepreneur. He's sending me to Disney World next week"

"Is that so?"

"Yes Miss Wallace. It's so...First class. You should come and kiss her off...at the airport.

Charlie spoke up...To his grandmother's surprise. He was a bit rude.

"Come on Grandmom let's take our seat."

This is why he was late. He couldn't tolerate the double and triple meanings of their talk. It seemed so impure to him, especially at church. This is why he was late so he could skip this and get right to the sermon. Once in their seats it was still a ninety minute affair. The two or three songs to sing, the sick list, the dead list and the special meetings list. Then the choir selection, or two. Finally the preacher started to speak. First thing he did was crack for money. It was a long crack but at the end it was just a crack. After the plate passed he sat down as some deacons took the plate to a back room. Now the choir sang another song and the preacher got up again. This time he wanted money for the choir cause they needed new robes and the plate came around again. Now the choir was singing a happy song as the pitter patter of coins could be heard hitting the plate. Muhammad gave another five, his grandmother only gave a dollar. She had dropped her

*The Adventures of Muhammad Smith and The Million Man March*

envelope on the first go round. After all this time the preacher introduced another preacher who finally gave the sermon.

"If you will please open your bibles to..."

The thin sheets of paper could clearly be heard as people quickly tried to find the passage. Muhammad sat quietly as his grandmother fumbled with her bible. Muhammad sat oblivious to it all. His mind was on Stephanie and of possibilities past and present. A slow smile emerged on his face when the preacher said...

"LORD! Help us in our days of woe. The People Looked UP to the LORD and said LORD Help Us."

Before Rev could get to the Lord's answer Muhammad's mind was wondering yet again, with a smile. Yesterday on the desk was intense and quick visions of various angles and positions crept into his mind. The trip to New York, seeing Bill Cosby, the different nature of sex, now that he displayed a new confidence. His prayers had all been answered in the span of two weeks. There must be a God.

But God don't pay bills, at least not in this church. The plate came around again this time for the guest speaker. Mac gave another five. The first preacher got up and said a few amens, with great emotion.

"I want to thank the brother for a fine sermon on the benevolence of our lord. Can I get a a-men?"

"A-men"

The congregation chimed in.

"I said AMEN!"

"AMEN."

This time they tried.

"And the people looked up and said 'Lord help us in our days of woe'"

"Amen."

It was the usual chimers.

"Now let us rise in our benediction."

The congregation followed suit rising with hand raised in prayer.

"Lord as we leave your house of worship and love we pray that you watch over us in our times of need and our tales of woe. And for the brothers who find their way to Washington DC, lord we ask that you touch their hearts and temper their resolve Lord, to find a direction unto the glory of you our father. Give them safe travel lord so that they may return to us as men Lord. Let them see that with your love all things are possible lord. Lord, long live the spirit of the Million Man March. In Jesus name we ask."

And then as if on cue the congregation sang

"AAAAAAAAMENNNNNNNN."

Then everybody started shaking hands. Grandmom started the Sister Wallace thing with Sisters Mary, Jane, Harris, Harrison and Thomas too. The wait wasn't that long though and soon enough she fetched him for his car and they were gone.

"Now that wasn't so bad was it now."

"No Grandmom it wasn't that bad."

"Excellent, then you can come next week."

"Actually Grandmom I already have a date for next week. Thanks all the same."

"A date with a girl?"

He had to admit it.

"Yes Grandmom, a date with a girl."

"Bring her to church. She'll enjoy it so much."

"Grandmom I think you're losing your touch."

"Oh I still got a trick or two up my sleeve. Did you see the young lady behind us? That's Sister Thomas' little girl. She just finished college you know."

"That's nice Grandmom but with two million in the bank, I'm not quite in need of a blind date."

"So where did you meet this mystery woman?"

"It's someone I already knew. I'll show her to you soon enough, don't worry."

She would of never guessed that her grandson would be falling in love with Stephanie Morgan all over again.

********

In Chicago and New Orleans buses rolled from parking lots, churches and bus depots. Black men were leaving the Mississippi valley in trains, planes and automobiles. Maybe they were a hundred to a bus or one in a car. They were leaving, knowing little more than they were going to listen to perhaps the most racist man in America and by the mere fact of their presence giving him credibility. The anticipation of the trip and the arrival in DC had a magical calming effect on everything. Police chiefs across America would realize in a few days that this weekend and especially Monday had the lowest crime rates than any other day in anyone's memory. But that was hindsight, in reality vacations were canceled for every gun carrying police officer in the metro DC area. While Black America was preparing for a day of atonement, White America was preparing for war. Most of the passengers on the buses were members of bars, churches and neighborhood associations who loosely knew each other before the trip. From the few indications that Muhammad could get it was starting to appear as if the bus trip in and of itself was a party for these 60,000 passengers. He wondered if it was like this for everybody. He thought for sure there had to be one city between LA and Chicago that had a blow out. Where temperatures boiled over or somebody stepped on someone's toe. Even he had to remind himself that the Muslims were too disciplined to allow such uncontrolled, spontaneous violence. Their violence was always very planned. There would only be one arrest during the so-called march on Washington. The buses were rolling from everywhere west of the Mississippi. People were singing, giving personal testimony of their lives in both Christian and non-Christian environments. In private conversations with strangers they talked of Rodney King, Rawanda, and two White girls named Susan Smith and Nicole Brown. They spoke of the Oklahoma City Bomb: The White man had raised the stakes again. Even the recent bombing in Arizona was quickly placed under the carpet with the words "Sons of the Gestapo". They spoke to what they thought to be the very definition of Black. Much of it was about being equal.

Muhammad never agreed with this line of thought. It was engrained in him every time he saw or heard the words "First Black Person to be...white." Once, after he heard the magical sermon of good and evil at the age of fifteen, he stumbled upon a statement on the radio. "The goal should have been a new bus company, not a equal seat on a bus in Montgomery." Nonetheless he was glad when Stephanie told him Rosa Parks was coming to the march. Even after she got mugged she still actually liked being Black. There must be a god.

It was the same old thing, the feelings were too intense, he couldn't bring himself to call Stephanie. Perhaps later in the evening. After all they would definitely see each other tomorrow morning. They would be leaving together in a customized bus made for a Rock and Roll band that went broke. Walter Peters from Mercury got it for him. There were chairs, beds, a bar and a bathroom with a shower. There would be enough of her tomorrow. Really he was a bit overwhelmed by her sudden attraction. During her whole serenade of "I love you" he couldn't bring himself to say the same, not once. Regardless of the mixed feelings of a long lost love there was too much to do. He had to call the independent bus companies for one final check. Once they realized that he wanted the buses for the Million Man March many of the White owners tried everything they could to break the contracts. In talking to them not only did Muhammad promise to take them to court if the buses weren't in place he also promised to set up picket lines in front of their businesses and homes. With the intensity of the current Black unity they didn't dare call his bluff, even though they were just as scared of their firm belief that one way or the other the Million Man March was a riot waiting to happen. The Black bus owners couldn't wait to go and once they realized the buses were for the march some of them even offered discounts. Muhammad gladly took them up on their offer. Finally he called Walter Peters of Mercury Bus Incorporated.

"Mr. Smith, or have you now decided on Mr. Muhammad?"

*Anonymous*

"Good day to you too Mr. Peters...Any problems, concerns?"

"One or two Mr. Smith, but you have no need to worry. I have my own motives. Every thing is running smooth, real smooth. How do you like the private bus I got you?"

"It's nice. Thank you."

"Get on that bus Mr. Smith and await the brave words of Mister Farrakhan."

"You know man I never got you. Why is this a big deal for you? I mean you got a good job, you can pass for white. What's the big deal?"

"Perhaps the pictures in my office don't reveal a son who doesn't want to be Black or a father who could never understand a child who preferred Louis Armstrong to Frank Sinatra."

"Yeah, everybody got problems."

"The millennium approaches Mr. Smith, I fear Farrakhan is your last chance."

"My last chance. Last chance for what?"

"Forget it Mr. Smith. Have a nice trip.

"I never got you man. Never."

Stevie was tying up the loose ends of a dope deal for Tuesday while Pee Wee could only think to look at Star Wars for a third time on TV. Stephanie waited by the phone and Raheem was studying Trigonometry III at Timothy's apartment on South Broad Street. But everybody got a good night's sleep.

# Meathead: ARCHIE BUNKER

3:00 AM the alarm clock went off and up he rose. The beginning of Monday, October 16th, 1995 had begun. He had to go to the bathroom, take a shower and then shave. So it began. First there was a call for Stephanie.

"So good morning Stephanie Morgan. How are you on this day of atonement?"

"If atonement means that I love you, then I'm fine Muhammad."

"…So are you ready, were there any issues yesterday."

"No, your Mercury people are great and I haven't seen this much unity since 1969. But it doesn't matter if the world is a storm Muhammad, I love you."

"So I take it you're ready to go. You know it's set for Progress Plaza at six."

"I still think that's too early Muhammad."

"The traffic will be heavy, real heavy. So are you ready?"

"I'm not going."

"Wait a minute take me back to 80 seconds ago when you said you love me."

"Muhammad this is a Black MAN thing. You go and listen to Farrakhan. I'll be waiting here at home for you. I'll follow you anywhere Muhammad but today you go to your Million Man March. This is a Farrakhan production so you go and pay your dues but I going to say this one more time, I'll say it a million times: I love you Muhammad."

"...I'll be back Stephanie...I feel for you."

With that he hung up. The day had begun. The Black Boy Scouts in Pittsburgh were well on their way.

He drove to the Fast Food Delite at Broad and Fairmount and parked in front. It was 5AM. From here he walked north on Broad until a C bus came along which he caught to Broad and Jefferson Streets. The sight was a tad overwhelming. A mass of perhaps a thousand, maybe two thousand men, women and children. The buses, his buses, were lined neatly in the parking lot and along Broad Street. And the crowd was so orderly that they were almost friendly. The group leaders of various organizations that had rented the buses monitored the perfectly orderly crowd. It was too easy. No one here knew that this slight, ex-fast food manager who walked amongst them had coordinated the buses that would deliver them to their amazing destination with an All-American profit. They were all having fun in their unity, the whole crowd was in one great big jovial and happy mood at 5:00 in the morning. "What could top this?" The thought repeated itself in his mind. "What could top this?"

There were children running to cars to pick up last minute food and cassette tapes. Women kissed their husbands, sons and brothers off with a pat on the

*The Adventures of Muhammad Smith and The Million Man March*

back and good tidings. The men fell into instantaneous conversations with strangers of all social status along with their girlfriends and children beside them. There were no paper bags, no aroma of marijuana, no petty arguments over a cigarette. What was happening? Why were all these people so happy. A church had set up a breakfast table and all comers were welcome. There were some hucksters selling T-shirts and glow in the dark yo-yo's but even at ten bucks a shirt, these folks had one goal in mind, get to Washington. For Muhammad his goal was met…He dared not call his bank account. The responses were starting to scare him.

Stevie had just woken up and was still more than an hour away from leaving. His gold tooth was still in his mouth and his Jerry curl was matted into a greasy pillow. James and his fellow republicans were dressed and packing their bus at 5 o'clock. By six they were at the Delaware state line. This was going to be a long trip.

Muhammad's bus was just where Peters said it would be, standing alone in front of the Mellon Bank. He walked up, through the crowd and to the bus with the multi color letters reading "The Clocks". He knocked on the door and they opened wide and a step above the ground. It was an old 60 year-old white bus driver.

"Are you Mr. Muhammad Smith?"

"The one and only."

"May I see your ID sir? My boss doesn't want any nonsense."

He smiled and reached for his wallet.

"Here you go."

"Thank you very much Mr. Smith as soon as your party arrives we can go per the boss's instructions."

*Anonymous*

"I think there won't be anyone else but me today Mr., Mr???"

"Robonski, Paul Robonski at your service."

"Mr. Robonski, just who is your boss?"

"Walter Peters, I'm his personal driver. Now please if you have no more questions and have all your things we can be on our way."

"How long will it take us to get there?"

"Please step behind the yellow line sir. Federal law dictates I can not move this bus until all parties are behind the yellow line."

Muhammad stepped behind the line and took a seat in a large recliner of a seat up front and close to the driver but behind the yellow line.

"We'll be taking the back roads today sir. An extra 30 minutes but traffic should be at a minimum. The icebox beside you is full of refreshments and you are welcome to watch television on any one of the four monitors throughout the bus. We also have a stereo system along with a library of cassette recordings."

With that Robonski pulled out of the parking lot leaving behind many of the other buses and the crowd surrounding them. Muhammad tuned the radio to KYW, 1060 and listened to the sports. The Braves were winning again. From his window Muhammad watched the crowd almost vibrate with a calm joy...Life if you will. Progress Plaza in Black North Philadelphia would never see such life again.

Robonski took 95 down to Chester County and then diverted to an obscure state road with almost no traffic at all. They took this road all the way through Delaware and on to the Maryland state line. It was 7:30

*The Adventures of Muhammad Smith and The Million Man March*

AM and they were just inside of Maryland. The view and the TV screens made for a relaxing ride. It was obvious this Robonski guy knew what he was doing.

"You come down here often Mr. Robonski."

Muhammad finally broke the silence.

"I've been coming to Washington for more than 30 years. My first trip was the King march back in nineteen hundred and sixty three. I was the driver for Reverend Sullivan and his church."

"You mean Mt. Zion."

"Yes that would be the one Mr. Smith. I always drove for Mt. Zion. Funny thing is, is that Mr. Sullivan said the King march inspired him to build the Plaza. But that march was integrated. He had the whites helping him. Probably the communists."

"You make it sound like J. Edger was a hero."

"In my opinion J. Edger Hoover was the greatest American that ever lived."

"FDR, Gee Washington even Johnny Appleseed?"

"George Washington had his war but FDR was a socialist who tried to eliminate the Supreme Court. Now J. Edger Hoover, J. Edger Hoover stood on the front lines of the war on Communism through two world wars, Korea and Vietnam. A real American."

Robonski pointed his eye and stuck his finger in the air. He was for real.

"So where are you from Mr. Robonski?"

To change the subject.

"I was born in Philadelphia in 1932 and I moved to Darby in nineteen hundred and sixty nine."

"Hmm, you like Darby?"

"I did but I'm moving to Downingtown after I retire. Too many niggers."

*Anonymous*

Robonski drove with a straight face. Eyes on the road, he knew what he said."

"Is that a fact?"

"Blacks move in, I move out. That's my policy."

"Makes for a better America hunh."

"I know you don't like my views Mr. Smith but they're the loudest ones on the block. Even on Easter, their cousins, aunts and friends. Even on Easter they're the loudest house on the block. And always, in every neighborhood, there's always one girl who wants to know. One white princess who wants to be savaged by a beast."

He grimaced and quickly composed himself.

"I have two daughters Mr. Smith. A man has to protect his future."

"I see."

"Any questions Mr. Smith?"

"Does the word racist mean anything to you Mr. Robonski?"

"Things were better when people were racist like your Malcolm X and your George Wallace. They got things done. But their own kind did 'em in. Today nobody's racist and nothing gets done. And Mr. Peters said you were the one for straight talk."

"What did Peters say?"

"That word doesn't work with me Mr. Smith."

"What?"

"Racist. That word doesn't scare me at all. That is the one thing that me and Mr. Peters agree on. Almost everybody is racist. He says that since your Mr. George Washington no one respected outside of their neighborhood has ever admitted they were racist. Mr.

*The Adventures of Muhammad Smith and The Million Man March*

Peters says that everyone in America is racist. For a White man my boss has strange ways Mr. Smith."

"Please no more Mr. Smith, I get enough of that with Peters. Call me Charlie."

"Yes sir Mr. Charlie."

"No, just Charlie."

"Whatever you wish sir."

"…Did you watch the King speech."

"Excuse me."

"The Martin Luther King speech, did you see it live when you drove Sullivan down?

"No but I saw it on TV that night. Bus drivers have to stay with the bus, it's company policy. Greatest speech I ever saw. Those nineteen minutes did a lot for your people Mr. Smith."

"Oh my people."

Robonski corrected himself.

"You know what I mean. The whole non-violence, day of service thing. A great thing for your people.

This will be my last trip today, I'm retiring. I asked Mr. Peters if I could go special. So he gave me this bus and told me to take you to this march thing."

"So your career starts and ends driving Black people to Washington"

"Ain't that the American way?"

Muhammad had no answer to this and Robonski drove.

Robonski took the ramp back onto the interstate and the traffic began to increase. From the perch of his recliner Muhammad could see hundreds of Black men through the windows of their cars and buses, all of them in conversation. Sometimes jovial, sometimes serious but they were all talking to one another. He could only guess at what they were talking about. For now his conversation was limited to a retiring White Pollock.

"What went wrong Mr. Robonski? How come we need another march?"

"Mr. Peters talks about it all the time. He says the Blacks never admitted that they were racist and that the very definition of the word racist became a mockery. He says that every conversation about race is a lie."

"A mockery of what?"

"Justice I suppose. I never thought about it, after all I'm not a racist. I do believe in Civil Rights."

"Is that what Hoover said?"

"The boss is always right Mr. Smith."

Just that quick they were off of the interstate and on the back roads of the Maryland countryside. They drove through suburban Maryland, bypassing Baltimore and all it's traffic. At about 8:30 Muhammad was on a bed in the rear of the bus taking a little catnap. Robonski drove down a deserted country road to a green sign with an arrow that read "495 WEST". Once Robonski climbed that ramp there was real traffic. Most of it was buses and cars full of Black Men still laughing their way to the Million Man March. The rest of the traffic was the routine commuter traffic. Those drivers, surprisingly almost all white and driving alone, were steamed and pissed off. This march had turned horrendous traffic into intolerable traffic. Many of these commuters could be seen pounding their dashes and steering wheels in frustration. This was the first thing Muhammad saw when he awoke from the steady country drive to the jerky stop and go of the interstate. The very sight of happy Black men next to angry White men gave him a certain joy. But there was nothing racist going on. He took the front recliner seat and watched the road ahead. He saw the sign for RFK stadium.

"That's where we're going, the stadium. Mr. Peters got reservations for the whole fleet."

It was all so easy. Robonski flashed some credentials to the guard and drove onto the field. There were hundreds of other buses but the order and lack of chaos for a crowd so large was amazing. At RFK stadium the FOI stood as ushers directing all men to the subway entrance. There was no need to read directions or instructions for the subway. It was as easy as following the crowd. Buy ticket for the train, get off at the Capitol station and walk onto a manicured large grass expanse bordered by the US Capitol building and the Washington Monument peppered heavily with Black men casually dressed in every hue, fashion and style. There were vendors selling food, water and T-Shirts. It was 9:25 AM, by three that afternoon they would all be sold out of everything. He walked on the steps that greeted the western entrance of the Capitol. Though only a few steps maybe 100 yards from the building itself, the steps were solid with statues adorned with strong lamp posts that were easy to climb and various people of all ages did just that. With each passing minute everyone figured this to be the spot to be at as it was so close to the speakers stand. But it got too crowded for Muhammad's taste and he moved to the middle of the mall past the second pair of large video monitors that stood on either side of the National Mall. In walking he heard little mumbles looking for the show to start. It was almost 10 o'clock and only introductory music was being played of African Drums. He walked with a certain confidence, which hid his shock, awe and satisfaction that things had gone so well, so massively. A stranger walked up to him and asked…

"Where are we marching to?"

"I don't think we're going anywhere, I'm just glad that a million guys showed up." Muhammad's answer wasn't good enough and the stranger asked the next passerby the same question. Muhammad just kept walking. To his left he saw the red brick building that he knew was the Smithsonian Institute from childhood trips to Washington. This is where he would stand when the first speaker spoke. A courteous fellow who explained where the toilets and first aid stations were. He also carefully explained there were booths where you could register to vote in all fifty states. The Republicans lead by Newt Gingrich had taken Washington with the lowest Black voter turnout since 1960. Then a guy came up who said that people were too close to the podium and that the crowd would have to move back and like a wave of water the crowd instantly obeyed his request and Muhammad could literally feel the surge of the crowd disperse throughout the large grassy field. Armies couldn't ask for such obedience. These men were thirsting for something. Something far more than the massive and gigantic video screens and the ceremonious precision of the Fruit Of Islam. Far more than the show that was meant to be, the show that really was, was the massive amount of people who wanted to be taken by the hand and lead. Already it was 10:30 and it seemed that the same guy was saying the same thing over and over again about the toilets, and the water and the voting. All around him though he enjoyed the sight of men talking with strangers. Even the sight of various, anonymous men bending down to pick up trash was a show, a rare show: Unity amongst one million men. In the weeks that followed these very men, and their cousins left behind, would crowd into churches and community centers, often overflowing out of the doors, for predetermined meetings, searching almost begging for leadership.

There was a murmur through the crowd that the official program was to begin at eleven. Eleven o'clock came and went. Still toilets, first aid and voting came from the podium. In his whole life, since the age of nineteen Muhammad had only missed voting once when they changed the voting place and he was two minutes late and he had learned first aid in the Army. This was getting old.

Then Stevie Wonder spoke to the crowd. A buzz of excitement went through the crowd. He was the first celebrity it seemed. And beyond this he was an undisputed poet laureate of his generation. What he did with words will live throughout history, without doubt. This is why Muhammad was so surprised that in his short, short speech the best he could say was "all for one and one for all." He was surprised but he accepted it. After all it was a valid message. Muhammad just expected more from Little Stevie. Soon it was Rosa Parks at the podium. Just seeing her alive was a thrill. She almost looked no older now than she did on the bus back in 1956. But the thought could never leave his mind that she was mugged by a Black man. Maya Angelou appeared with the official start of the "March" with a poem. She read her poem with reverence, dignity and several big words but there was nothing memorable.

*Anonymous*

Then began a string of various dignitaries from Black, Colored, Negro and African-American America. All giving short, scheduled speeches repeating the same themes over and over again: Unity, responsibility and the endless plea for equality in opportunity such as Black football coaches, in 1995. Every now and then there was the classic "White man done me wrong". There was the crass such as Gus Savage, a former congressman from Chicago, who said that Black men were not angry enough at White America. Then there was the classy Jessie Jackson, also of Chicago, who claimed that Farrakhan didn't organize the March but rather it was the policies of Clarence Thomas and Newt Gingrich that created the March. 'Cute' Muhammad thought. But of them all Muhammad was most impressed with a 14 year-old boy named Ayene Baptiste.

"Your sons and daughters will no longer need to belong to gangs because they do belong…Our youth will no longer be seeking drugs as an escape because there will be outlets in our society to develop themselves… our enemies can destroy us one by one. But nobody can stop one million men organized."

Perhaps the surprise of the day was the presence of Betty Shabazz, the widow of Malcolm X. She spoke of a redefinition of values and goals. The job of a leader. A job her husband was well on his way to performing until he was shot. A few years later their daughter would be arrested for the attempted murder of Louis Farrakhan. It was quickly forgotten by the White media, the Black Media and the law. The truth of Malcolm X like the truth of the Alamo is best left unsaid.

*The Adventures of Muhammad Smith and The Million Man March*

Still the repeated short speeches extolling the virtues of unity and responsibility were beginning to get old. The crowd began to chant:

"Farrakhan, Farrakhan, Farrakhan".

When that didn't work they elaborated their intentions:

"We want Farrakhan, we want Farrakhan, we want Farrakhan…"

It was approaching 4 o'clock, the scheduled end of the 'March'. Muhammad needed a phone. The buses were scheduled to leave at 5PM. He needed to get in touch with Stephanie. She would know what to do. Cell phones were rare in 1995 and every phone booth within three blocks had a line. Not that Muhammad had walked the three blocks but seeing the half block lines at every public phone for a block Muhammad knew it was worthless to walk another two blocks. He picked a public phone and pulled out a wad of cash and gave everyone in the line five dollars to let him jump. For some groups of four he gave a twenty, they had to get their own change. He walked down the line until one guy demanded 10 dollars.

"Nigger please."

And Muhammad kept walking.

Getting to the phone he used his phone card and called Stephanie at the office. "Please be there, please be there." It was dawning on him that this was an emergency. The phone rang in Philadelphia and in his ear. The phone remained in it's tiny place on Miss Harris' desk with Muhammad's ear pressed to the receiver of a public phone in Washington DC. Suddenly a hand reached for the Philly phone.

"I.S.I.S. Mrs. Harris speaking."

*Anonymous*

"Miss Harris, it's me Muhammad is Stephanie there?"

"Hello young fella, how are…"

"Miss. Harris I need to talk to Stephanie now."

"Wait right here, I'll be right back."

She put the receiver down and ran her over aged body to the women's bathroom.

"Miss Morgan, I got Muhammad on the line he wants to talk to you bad."

In the stall Stephanie quickly pulled up her jeans and ran for the phone past Mrs. Harris…

"Hello, Muhammad?"

"Am I glad to hear from you. This thing is running past 4 0'clock. No way it's going to end by five."

"Muhammad these bus companies are going to charge double if you don't leave by five. They're starting to call now."

"It's a lie. They're scarred to be here after dark."

"But it's in the contract Mac."

There was silence as Muhammad looked down the long line for the public phone. But Farrakhan still hadn't spoken. He couldn't abandon Farrakhan…It was the reason for everything. This would be his sacrifice for the cause…A million bucks.

"Listen I'll call you back in thirty minutes."

"Mac I need to know by 4:30."

"I'll call Stephanie, I'll call."

He hung up the phone and walked back into the crowd on the mall. As luck would have it he passed the Black Boy Scouts. They were pooped with half of them asleep on the lawn. The crowd still chanted for Farrakhan when suddenly a cheer went through a million Black men. It was Farrakhan on the giant monitors, approaching the podium...Finally. The cheers subsided and finally he spoke. Somewhere along the way someone from the podium asked for a dollar from every brother. Muhammad pulled out his checkbook from his ever present blazer and wrote a check for one thousand dollars and put it in the brown paper bag that made it's way through the crowd. Then there was a brief statement of a cure for AIDS but no one listened.

"In the name of Allah..."

And so it began, the climax of the Million Man March. Farrakhan began by thanking Farad, Elijah, Benjamin Chavis and Dr. Dorothy Height of the National Council of Negro Women. This was expected but what came next was beyond belief. Without missing a beat there was talk of various numbers derived by various methods that meant various things. Once, long ago, Muhammad had heard the word numerology but he never thought he would see such a thing. He quickly went back to the public phone past the sleeping Black Boy Scouts.

"Two dollars a minute, make your calls for two dollars a minute."

It was a huckster with a primitive cell phone that had a battery the size of a brick. One look at the line for the pay phone and Muhammad knew a good deal when he saw one. Giving the brother a twenty Muhammad called Stephanie with one message.

"We leave at five."

Stepping back into the crowd he watched as messengers and bus stewards spread the word one by one: The buses were leaving and so were the people.

Listening to the speech Muhammad heard tales of confession, the Bible and the Koran. But at this point Muhammad didn't care if Orgena spelled Negro backwards or Black sideways, he was leaving. It was his clearest thought all day: This was no 19 minutes of "I have a dream". The trip on the Metro seemed shorter or perhaps it's that there seemed to be more happening on the train than at the March. The subway was full of brothers still in conversation, still together, but the unity was just a tad bit less. Leadership is such an ill-defined and rare commodity. Back on the bus he and Robonski had nothing to talk about so he retired to the rear tuning the radio to find the rest of the speech. It went on for two and a half hours. The sentences were deep and perhaps full of meaning but just as he honed in to a deeper meaning the subject would take another metaphysical jump. Yes there were history lessons, full of tales of woe and the wisdom of heaven but somewhere in the middle of this speech the words of Maya Angelou rotated in Muhammad's mind:

"The night has been long,

The wound has been deep,

The pit has been dark,

And walls have been steep"

He didn't know what it meant, it just rotated. Having to tune the radio through several cities he was exhausted from listening so hard and when it got to the part about pledging to come to work on time he was glad it was over. By now Robonski and his back door routes had them well into Delaware. Soon he would be home.

*********

*The Adventures of Muhammad Smith and The Million Man March*

James was still jammed up on I-95 North while Stevie was stuck in DC. Muhammad was home. He was tired. A call to Stephanie would have been nice but he had been up since 3 o'clock that morning. It was now near eleven. It was the best sleep he had had in a long time.

A year would pass before hindsight would kick in, though from the beginning it was obvious. The next day there was controversy over the official size of the crowd. It was placed at 400,000. Then some scientist guy scientifically deduced that the size of the crowd was between 1.1 to 1.5 million people. Within a week the official count was changed to .8 to 1.1 million people. They, the official counters, had underestimated the Black men by 50%. This seemed to prove the whole point.

Within that same week every building capable of hosting five or more people in every Black neighborhood in America was packed with Black men and often women anxious to help, volunteer, donate, participate, anything. Muhammad himself joined a voter registration drive in Germantown. Then one week he blinked his eyes and the Muslims were gone. Fortunately for the voting committee in Germantown it was run by a cranky old lady, who wore a Khimar but she never changed her name. When the church was no longer available she held meetings in her house, which sorta was in Nicetown, but nice none the less. They lasted until the primary the following May. Muhammad deposited a thousand dollars into a new Million Man March Bank. He never saw the money again. There

*Anonymous*

were reasons and explanations but the money would never add up. Oddly enough perhaps the biggest story of public success, both Negro and White, during this whole Rodney King, Susan Smith, Oklahoma City and OJ thing was a Collegiate Lacrosse All Star who quite obviously didn't go to the Million Man March and was, is the Blackest Man in America: Jim Brown. His drive to end gang violence and culture in LA was a valid success, though they soon found other reasons to kill each other. A year later OJ Simpson was still with a White woman golfing at golf courses around the country, though not at the plush greens of the Country Clubs of Chicago. It had gone by so quickly, this million man thing. Where was the answer? Was there an answer?

A year later on the slopes of the hills in the south of France, Muhammad picked up a copy of "America Today". It was a few days old but it was the USA. Though not quite a year, the paper had published a story reporting on the MMM, "A Year Later". He read the story over several times. Two statements, from two different individuals pictured it so well, diversity if you will. Kirby Alexander said "The people who put it together were accomplished people who became part of the system. They didn't want change."

Then in another city Terry Smith said "The reality of the march is probably small steps. If people keep taking them they will have the greatest impact." Again, there in the south of France, the words came back to him:

"The night has been long,
The wound has been deep,
The pit has been dark,
And the walls have been steep."

# GUNSMOKE

Pee Wee got out of bed at his leisure at about nine o'clock. All of the good cartoons were off. It was his birthday so now he was eleven. He had been taking his own baths since the age of four. He couldn't spell bath to save his life but every couple of days he would break out the beads and really relax. It was one of his lifelong pleasures. He put on yet another new set of clothes along with his prize Nikes. He would never know it but it was his sudden change of wardrobe that helped hide him from the cops. He bopped down the steps into the sparse living room floor where his mother, Mary, was laying yet again in the lap of another hooded stranger. She was still sleep. He made his way to the kitchen, opened the ice box for the routine exasperation. Nothing but crumbs from last night's take out dinner and an orange juice bottle full of water. "I'll be back ma." The moan she gave wasn't worth a response. He left.

Stephanie was at her office on time, she knew better than Muhammad that there would be calls with complaints from the riders and the bus companies. She was presently surprised to find that almost everyone was exhausted from Monday. Tuesday turned out to be a relatively calm workday until Muhammad came in.

"Good Morning Miss Morgan."

"Mr. Muhammad, surprise, surprise."

"There's no surprise Stephanie. I told you I would be here."

"I figured you for the sleep at home type."

"Army training, you figured wrong."

With that he was upon her with a kiss, the warm embracing kind. She was always the professional.

"Mac, Mac we got work to do."

"Oh."

He released her.

"But we can do lunch at Becky's."

"That sounds good."

"Now get on the phone and call the independents. Make sure the buses got back in one piece, alright."

He nodded his head. "Well alright."

Steven Livingston was out cold. He didn't make it back to Philly until 3 AM. He insisted on seeing the Chocolate City sites and got stuck in the 11 PM traffic jam instead of the 5 o'clock traffic jam. It was 9 o'clock so he still had another couple of hours before his afternoon appointment. At the March he stood through the whole speech almost literally saying "Right On" one thousand, four hundred and seventy nine consecutive times. When it was over he found a fancy hotel bar and managed to have a good time even though he was the only Black at the bar. He dazzled them.

"And then I said, I said...Nigger Puhleese. You know what I'm sayin'. "

There was one Harvard lookin' white dude in the corner who seemed to analyze Stevie's every word. It was funny and scary at the same time. Especially when he tried to decipher "Nigger Puhleese".

Pee Wee found his way to downtown thinking he could sneak in and see the R Rated flick "Dead Presidents". It was at the RiVue Cineplex on Delaware Avenue. He got lost, he was hungry and he was late. The movie started at 12 noon and he got there at 12:30, another two hours before the next show. Aside from the movie theater there was nothing on Delaware Avenue but a dirty river and a Pep Boys Auto parts store. He caught a bus which took him west to Broad Street instead of north to Center City. It didn't matter because the first thing he had to do was eat. And Broad Street had plenty of Cheesteak shops. He ordered one with extra cheese but the shop didn't have change for a fifty dollar bill. The story was the same at the next steak shop. By now he was close enough to Center City that he decided to wait, after all everyone downtown was rich, change for a fifty would be a snap.

"Raheem is coming, his classes were canceled for some teacher's conference or something. I told him two o'clock."

Muhammad turned quiet.

"I wish I never took that blood test Stephanie. I'm sorry they even invented a blood test. I should of stayed with you then. I should…"

She put her finger to his lips.

"Muhammad, that's over. Today we're going to go to Becky's and enjoy a good fish dinner. OK."

"OK."

He was up now picking at his Jerry Curl complete with gold tooth. The mirror didn't lie. He called Larry. Everything was set, a hundred grand. He went for the closet, opened the door and pulled the attaché case. On the bed he turned the combination and opened the lid to a neat, tightly packed row of clear plastic bags full of "white gold". He stepped to the door with a certain pep to his step and the attaché case. Today he would be going first class in his Beamer. Dope deals were fun.

Pee Wee made it downtown and finally got his Cheesteak with extra cheese. The steak guy cheated him in a bad way. Not only did he outright take several dollars from the eleven year-old child but he didn't even give him the forty nine cents change.

"Here's your change, forty five dollars sir."

Actually it was eight five dollar bills but Pee Wee put it right into his pocket.

"Fried Onions with that sir?"

"Yeah and hot sauce too."

He ate well inside the restaurant not quite aware of the time. None the less his hunger was satisfied. Leaving he thought to ask…

"What time is it."

"It's one thirty kid."

"How much longer for two o'clock?"

The shop owner couldn't believe his ears and looked at the 'innocent' child.

"Thirty minutes kid."

Pee Wee didn't think to say thank you. He just left, in a slight rush.

*The Adventures of Muhammad Smith and The Million Man March*

Raheem hadn't arrived yet. It was only the two of them Stephanie and Muhammad alone at Becky's best table in front, next to the cash register with a view of Fairmount Avenue.

"You know that I'm with someone right? She lives with me. It won't be easy."

"First I lose out to a drug dealer now I lose out to your girl friend."

"Mac, don't get dramatic. I want to be with you. I don't want to argue. OK?"

With a sudden smile "OK."

"Hey mom."

"Raheem!"

He gave the expected, but loving kiss to the cheek.

"Hello Mr. Smith."

"Raheem, it's Mr. Muhammad."

"That's ok Stephanie, I kinda like Mr. Smith."

"Sit down and get a menu. Let's spend some of Mr. Muhammad's money."

"Yes Mam."

It was like a family.

Stevie parked his car just west of the AutoShop Bar and Grill. Had he but looked just east of the café he would of seen his childhood friends and perhaps of made it to old age. Today he would walk into the bar of a friend to make his biggest dope deal ever. This would be real money. He cut the almost pure cocaine from New York and was set to multiply his money greatly.

Pee Wee caught a bus but it was the wrong one. Everything was cool until the bus turned north. Before

*Anonymous*

he realized it was the wrong bus he was already at 22<sup>nd</sup> and Fairmount. He got off but now he needed change. All he had was fives. There was a store, a restaurant it looked black. The bar next to it looked white. He was a kid, what did he know.

"Mom, I'll be back, I'm going to the bathroom"
He walked the short distance to the men's room in a side hall, next to the register.
"He's grown well Steph, you did a good job."
"My parents had their say. It was a community effort. And who was the love of your life."
"You say that word like it's so common. I missed out on the love part Stephanie. It doesn't work for me.
"Oh."

Stevie whispered to the bartender who pointed to a back room. He knocked on the door.
"Yeah who is it?"
"It's me man, Stevie the candy man."
The door opened, it was Larry.
"Come on in brother. Mi Casa Su Casa."
Stevie stepped in with the attaché case.
"Hey pea you got the cash?"
Stevie wanted to make this quick.
"It's cool bro, it's cool. You want a drink man."
"Give me a CC and Seven with a hundred grand on the side."
"You got the dope?"
"Got the dope? What do I look like, a dope? Of course I got the dope. Do you got the money nigger?"
"Alright Stevie relax. You know this is my first time, I mean how does this work? Do I give you the money

*The Adventures of Muhammad Smith and The Million Man March*

and then you give me the dope or do you give me the coke first? Am I gonna give you the money and then you say you'll be back. I mean how does it work?"

Pee Wee made his way across the street to Becky's. All he needed was change. He walked in attracting more attention than he was expecting. It was a Black restaurant and most of the Blacks were looking at him, a child in an adult restaurant during school hours with a pair of fancy shoes. He made his way to the register.
"Miss can I have change for a dollar."
He handed her the five.
"You mean change for a five don't you?"
"Lady I just need carfare. Can I have some change."
"Young man why aren't you in school? Where's your mother at..."

"Look, I'm gonna throw my stuff on this table, you go and get your cash and throw it down on the table and then we pick up what's ours. Cool?"
"Cool."
Stevie slapped the case on the table, turned the combo and opened it for all to see, to include the camera in the ceiling. Larry reached for a draw.
"Careful with them quick moves buddy, now ain't the time."
He pulled out his new gun, just for show. Larry pulled out a paper bag full of stacks of money a total of ninety grand. He placed it on the table and Stevie picked up what was his.
"FREEZE FBI."

"By time the 'Z' had left the African American agent's lips he was shot and FBI was his last word. Stevie broke for the door over the agent's body. The other two agents fired so many bullets so quickly they could barely see for the smoke. Stevie was running through the bar, shot in the arm. It was dangling.

Pee Wee from next door could hear the shots, he panicked and she said the wrong thing. He shot that lady dead. Raheem was just out of the bathroom and heard all the shots so he ran to his mother.
"Mom!"
Stevie ran past the door for his life when he saw his childhood friends. He ran for them…idiocy.
"My mother ain't here!"
Pee Wee held the gun like Luke Skywalker with two hands and picked Raheem off like a monster from the planet Argon. Before he knew it there was a man behind him with a gun.
What could she do but scream.
"AAAAGGGGHHHHHHHH"
Muhammad could not believe it. He sat transfixed… petrified. It was Pittsburgh all over again. Was there nowhere on this planet. Then he saw Stevie.
In one glance Stevie understood the whole situation. Even right down to the educated guess that this kid was the miscreant who killed the teacher in the news and to include the fact that this child had just shot his son dead.
"Oh my god, oh my god."
He simply held his gun up and shot. He missed a few times and Pee Wee got him on the side of the stomach but Stevie just kept shooting and popped the

*The Adventures of Muhammad Smith and The Million Man March*

kid in the chest. The kid was down. But this wasn't enough, the chump had Stevie's gun!

"Oh my god. The nigger got my gun."

Stevie stood over the fallen child and continuously shot with a sense of rhythm. Then the rest of the FBI came.

Stephanie screamed again.

"AAAGGGGHHHHHHHH!!!!"

"PUT THE GUN DOWN LIVINGSTON!"

"He placed it to his head but never did make it. The FBI guys emptied their weapons on him. Through the smoke Stephanie ran to her child, dying on the floor. She knelt in the blood cuddling her only child.

"I really wanted to meet Mr. Muhammad mom."

For the rest of his life he would always remember the sight of her crying, alone, with that little dark baby.

The End